MAKING THE MODERN GARDEN

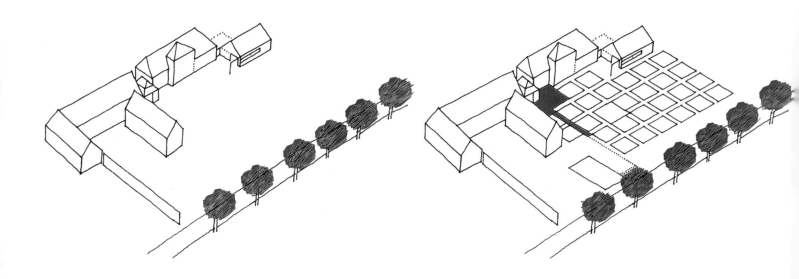

CHRISTOPHER BRADLEY-HOLE

MAKING THE MODERN GARDEN

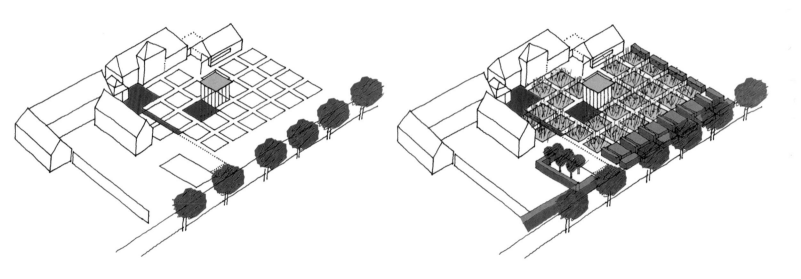

with MARK GRIFFITHS

THE MONACELLI PRESS

First published in the United States in 2007 by
The Monacelli Press, Inc.
611 Broadway, New York, New York, 10012

© Octopus Publishing Group Limited 2007

Library of Congress Cataloging-in-Publication Data
Bradley-Hole, Christopher.
Making the modern garden / Christopher Bradley-
Hole ; with Mark Griffiths.
p. cm.
Includes bibliographical references and index.
ISBN 978-1-58093-152-6 (hardcover)
1. Gardening. I. Griffiths, Mark, date. II. Title.
SB450.97.B734 2007
712—dc22   2007016324

Printed and bound in China

Half title: Detail from *Garden of the Desert,*
Chelsea Flower Show 2003, designed by
Christopher Bradley-Hole
Title page: Isometric plans of the garden
Hortus Conclusus, Chelsea Flower Show 2004, designed by
Christopher Bradley-Hole
Contents page: Detail from Elie Saab Chalet, I Faqra Club,
Lebanon, designed by Vladimir Djurovic

CONTENTS

INTRODUCTION

Modernism was a 20th-century movement – by the 1980s, artists, architects, and authors were already talking about Post-Modernism, as if that, too, had not long to go. So why, in the first decade of the 21st century, do I offer you a book titled, *Making the Modern Garden*?

The first reason is history. Modernism revolutionized gardens and landscapes much as it did the other arts. Both abstract gardens and abstract painting were subject to the same principles. For example, one of the most famous Modernist gardens was created in 1928 by Gabriel Guevrekian at Hyères in France. Here is a garden whose debt to modern painting is graphically obvious – a triangular grid of coloured squares, it is often called "The Cubist Garden".

Sometimes this symbiosis between the fine arts and the arts of the garden was even more seamless. Modernist architects such as Le Corbusier and Luis Barragán made gardens and landscapes that reflected their building designs. Sculptors as eminent as Barbara Hepworth and Isamu Noguchi made great gardens as adjuncts to and expressions of their art, as did the painter Patrick Heron, the film-maker Derek Jarman, and so gloriously on. Conversely, landscape artists such as Roberto Burle Marx were equally at home with other genres and media, seeing such endeavours as part of the same creative Modernist enterprise.

In *Making the Modern Garden*, I want to put the garden into a cultural context, to explore its part in the transformation of the arts that Modernism wrought, and to ask you to look at gardens and landscapes with the same expectations as you would bring to a painting, building, or sculpture. This is the book's historical function – to make a case for Flora joining the other modern Muses.

Now the second, and much more important, reason for producing a book on modern gardens well over half a century after Modernism might be thought to have climaxed. Quite simply, garden-makers have not finished with Modernism yet. In some ways – which I hope to show you – we have barely started with it. Although I have just alluded to a pantheon of modern masters who revolutionized garden and landscape in the last century, our green genre abounds in untapped potential for fresh experiments and departures. In this vast and still-expanding scope we garden-makers are fortunate. It would be difficult to say the same of modern painting or poetry.

One reason for this enduring potential is that Modernism and gardens are a perfect match. If we consider some of the keynote principles and props of modern garden design, such as abstraction from Nature, or the grid and enclosure, we find them not just in the present and the century past, but also in far more remote eras and cultures. For example, the temple of Ryoan-ji in Kyoto contains an enclosed landscape just 250sq m (2,700sq ft). It consists of a bed of raked pale gravel and 15 stones. The only plant is the moss that fringes the stones. Utterly simple yet conceived with consummate artistry, this landscape is an abstraction of Nature that evokes complex feelings and associations by a process of radical reduction. In this respect it is a modern garden, albeit 500 years old.

What Modernism offers us, then, is the distillation and synthesis of certain fundamentals of garden design. Couple these with new materials and technologies and a new spirit of exploration, and it becomes impossible to name any other period of horticultural history that has promised more diversity and innovation than the present. For the garden, the 21st century is the modern age. I, for one, feel excited and privileged to have arrived there at last.

When it first appeared in 1936, George Taylor's book *The Modern Garden* predicted big changes in horticultural fashion. In fact, those changes have become widely apparent only in recent years. Even now the modern garden remains *terra incognita* for some and liable to prompt misgivings. For example, to mark its bicentenary in 2004, the Royal Horticultural Society staged a debate in London. Underlying the motion of the debate, *This house believes that horticultural craft will determine the culture of the gardens of the future at the expense of artistic expression,* was a concern that "traditional" horticulture and ultra-modern design were incompatible and heading for a nasty divorce.

For me this spins on a false dichotomy. One can certainly be both a plant and a design person. Indeed, great modern design and great planting are not only compatible but sometimes inseparable. So the pages that follow amount to a plea, really, that we should overcome these anti-modern prejudices and allow the garden the same developmental sophistication that we are prepared to accept in other art forms. At the same time, I want to offer guidance on what to look for in modern gardens, where to find them, and how to make them.

From all of this a message emerges to solace those who worry that Modernism drives a barrier between design and horticulture. A garden does not need plants like a library needs books, but the influences of landscape and vegetation are a different matter. All gardens are informed by these. This relationship between Nature, culture, and cultivation is something I explore in this book. It is the big idea behind many contemporary designs, as it is now in the world beyond them. Little wonder that the modern garden, powerful and poetic, has become such a vital means of self-expression.

For the Chelsea Flower Show in 1997, I designed a Modernist garden inspired by the Roman poet Virgil. I believe that gardens can convey complex narratives, and my intention here was to engage the viewer in an exploration of the relationship between Nature, culture, and cultivation.

Making gardens should be a liberation, an opportunity for freedom of thought and expression. Yet far too often we find ourselves constrained by our common experience, by the familiar or comfortable, by what others have done and are doing. If these conservative influences inhibit our creativity, so too does the profusion of trends and novelties that the fashion-hungry media feed us. True innovation comes not from following the familiar or the voguish, but from knowing our roots and understanding why things are as they are.

In making gardens, we should look to the landscape first for inspiration. This, after all, is the root source of the materials from which gardens are made. In the civilized world there is little chance of finding a truly natural landscape unchanged by man. But we can learn from "cultured" landscapes. Still primitive, these are landscapes that have been changed for reasons far more fundamental and urgent than, say, decoration or amenity. Iron Age hill forts, for example, such as the one at Maiden Castle in Dorset, were defensive structures. On the success of their design depended life and death, no less.

Today, we sense that these sculpted landforms were strong concepts that employed the best talents of their time in the service of a critical need. The hill fort retains the power to communicate, to move us. Landscape also makes us aware of

Previous pages:
The pure form and rough texture of landscape sculptor Richard Long's *Brittany Red Stone Circle* captivate us, making us focus on a woodland scene and question our relationship with it. Would we be so aware of its wildness were a human artefact not at its centre? Garden makers also seek to explore the relationship between Nature and nurture, wild and cultivated.

Right:
Sculpted landforms such as Maiden Castle, the largest Iron Age hill fort in Britain, are models for our own, less dramatic interventions in the landscape.

natural cycles, ecosystems and plant adaptations. Plants growing in the wild can teach us how they would wish to be grown in gardens. To observe their habitats is also a stepping stone to using them creatively within the context of a garden. Natural plant communities indicate the character of the landscape that they occupy, as in the complex matrix of grasses and wild flowers that makes up a prairie or meadow. When we read that landscape, we do not see the plants in isolation but in concert. The composition of these communities and their relationship to their context have an essential rightness about them that can be reproduced when making gardens.

Landscapes can change dramatically with the seasons. For much of the year Namaqualand, in South Africa's Northern Cape, is arid and seemingly barren. Yet each spring this region hosts a staggering display of wild flowers stimulated by the winter rains. Their swathes of colour remind us of the power of plants to transform even a vast and hostile terrain. We experience a natural landscape like this one on two levels. There is the overall effect, the abstract pattern formed by the plants *en masse* when seen at a distance. Then there is the intimate association of the plants when viewed close up. When planting, we should bear both views in mind, aiming to create a garden that engages us both as a whole and in the intricacy of its detail.

Working with a change of level or on sloping ground presents a challenge and an opportunity in garden making. Here we can learn lessons from the way that some people have invented strategies that not only make working the land possible but also

Above:
Each spring the rugged landscape of Namaqualand, in South Africa's Northern Cape, comes alive with millions of wild flowers after the winter rains. These huge swathes of colour remind us of the power of plants to transform even hostile terrain. There is much to be learned from the patterns made by natural vegetation when designing plantings for the garden.

Above:
The rice terraces at Longsheng in China show how cultivation can sometimes enhance our appreciation of the natural landscape. The terraces allow us to read the slopes like a contour map, making it easier to understand the relationship of one hill to another.

result in remarkable transformed landscapes. Rice terraces on the steep hillsides of China demonstrate this link between compelling necessity and the ingenuity required to find a solution. Created using only primitive tools and bare hands, they stand today as examples of agriculture at its most radical. They are equally magnificent and enduring landmarks, no less dramatic than an Iron Age hill fort. Moreover, these beautiful terraces help me to understand the levels of the hillsides. Before their intervention it would have been more difficult to appreciate the relationship of one hill to another: the terraces explain the slopes and allow us to read them like a contour map. Similarly, I recall a field study by landscape students of the University of Weihenstephan in which they were asked to draw the contour lines in white chalk across the hilly landscape north of Munich. This simple experiment made a subtle but powerful statement and gave a new perspective on the lie of the land.

The Chinese rice terraces are just one instance among many of successful cultivation in the face of daunting conditions. It is easy to understand why people went to such lengths to feed themselves; but there are also examples of strictly non-essential cultivation undertaken in the teeth of adversity. The ancient gardens of the Middle East were made despite the barren landscape that surrounded them. They were protected from it by high walls – hence *hortus conclusus*, the "enclosed garden", one of the most fundamental garden types. Whereas everything outside the gardens was barren, chaotic, exposed, and arid, within the walls there was order, shade, water, and abundant planting. The enclosed garden concept endures as an emblem of the need to create and to cultivate wherever we are.

Gardens connect with us more profoundly than any other artistic endeavour. This is partly because they are constantly offering new points of connection, new aspects and insights, as they change with the elements and seasons, and with the hours and years. Their materials, likewise, are dynamic: plants grow; wood and stone weather. This is true even of gardens described as timeless – a Japanese moss garden, for example. The moss carpet itself is an illuminating paradox. Here is a floor, but not a floor for walking upon. It is, rather, a series of cushions or small valleys and mounds from which rocks and trees emerge. It evokes a double scale: at once a rolling landscape and a tiny quilt, macro and micro. There is also an emotional connection. The moss garden strikes us as rare, precious, and perfectly tended. But that, too, is a comment on the way our values and perceptions change: the moss arrived in this garden as a weed in the 19th century. Only later did this happy accident come to be revered as its greatest feature.

We can find inspiration for garden design from almost all sources. Gardens are statements about life and the sanctity of cultivation and development. When we make a garden we are getting in touch with soul and soil. We are not confining ourselves to the garden but making a comment on life and the qualities that are important to us. Garden-making should not be cut off from the rest of the world but central to it.

Some take the view that, because plants and wild habitats appear asymmetric or random, so too should our gardens. This opinion favours informal over formal, naturalistic over

Above:
Defended from the desert by high walls, the lush paradise at Bagh-e-Shahzadeh in Iran is an astonishing example of the *hortus conclusus*, one of the oldest garden types.

Left:
This Japanese moss garden in Kyoto works as a landscape in miniature, with slopes, gullies, and soaring crags. On a larger scale, it is a flawless canvas on which trees and rocks appear like a calligrapher's brushstrokes. Good garden design exploits both the detail and the overall atmosphere of plants and materials.

artificial – both distinctions that do not really bear scrutiny. "There are no straight lines in Nature", is commonly heard in support of this view; but is that right? For a start the horizon is straight, as is the unseen force of gravity. Plants themselves are replete with rectilinear and geometric patterns at almost every level, as are geological formations. In the man-made environment, we find straight lines in many of our buildings and cities. We seem prepared to accept those. Why should we be nervous about our gardens having a rational geometry?

As the primal garden was the enclosed *hortus conclusus*, so the basic structure within this garden geometry is the frame, the boundary. A garden is a place apart, but not divorced from its surrounds. If we think of it as a painting, then the best analogy is offered by the British artist Sir Howard Hodgkin whose paint often covers the frame as well as the area the frame encloses. Negotiating this relationship between content and context is one of the starting points of garden design. What follows is an example of that being done unconsciously but with great beauty.

En route to the Middle East, I always make a point of looking out of the window when flying over the Balkans and Turkey. As well as a vivid mountainous landscape, you see remarkable patterns made by fields laid out for agricultural production. From the air these fields read as a quilt of interlocking patches, some dark, some light, depending on which crops are being grown. When centred on a market town their shapes converge in an apparently ad hoc arrangement that, nonetheless, has an overriding logic. It is form following function – a perfect, if accidental, expression of Modernist ideas.

I take such found patterns as inspiration for garden layouts. What inspires me particularly about this example is the tension and contrast generated by the fields, which vary in size, shape, and content, as they meet head to head, touching each other within a grid. The effect is just like an abstract painting. Of course, that is not to endorse this kind of intensive farming. But what may not be best practice in terms of agriculture is still a powerful source of aesthetic ideas for horticulture. On a smaller scale, blocks of ornamental perennials could be organized on such a grid with similar drama. So we look to the landscape and the wider world when planning gardens.

The landscape has long been a source of fascination for artists and philosophers. One reason for this fascination is the philosophical issue of how we view Nature, both in reality and in idealized form, as in the concept of an Arcadian landscape. Arcadia

(actually in the central Peloponnese peninsula of Greece and of harsh and mountainous terrain) was portrayed in literature as an ideal landscape, gentle and fertile, home to shepherds and rustic deities. Classical authors developed this idea of the bucolic idyll, most notably the Roman poet Virgil in his *Eclogues* (37BC). In the Renaissance, it returned to enchant writers and artists, few of whom had any knowledge of Arcadia as an actual place. In the 17th century, painters such as Nicolas Poussin and Claude Lorrain subscribed to the Arcadian vision wholesale, depicting ideal landscapes rather than real ones. Their influential paintings were, in turn, adopted by writers as the very model of Nature herself and of a new type of garden that would pay homage to her.

One such writer was Uvedale Price, who commented in his *Essays on the Picturesque* (1810) that, "every person of observation must have remarked how broad the lights and shadows are on a fine evening in nature, or (what is almost the same thing) a picture of Claude [Lorrain]." Price's view of the real landscape was shaped by a long tradition of poems and paintings that exalted an imaginary landscape. In effect, Nature was seen to

Below:
The paintings of Claude Lorrain depict mythological subjects within mythological landscapes: as here, with Argus guarding Io, transformed into a heifer, in an imaginative reconstruction of Arcadia. This benign and decorous wilderness was an idea inherited from Classical Antiquity. From the 17th century onwards, it came to influence the ways in which we viewed Nature and attempted to improve on her in gardens.

be imitating art. Jean-Jacques Rousseau thought the English landscape came closest to the sacredness of Nature in her purest form. Other commentators, however, urged landscape gardeners to improve upon that form by adopting the paintings of Poussin and Claude Lorrain as models. Organized as journeys inspired by Classical mythology, English landscape gardens such as Stourhead and Stowe were Arcadia revisited. Within this Arcadian vision, garden and countryside were not necessarily distinct.

William Kent, one of the greatest designers of the 18th century, inspired the phrase "leaping the fence" when describing how he would open up gardens to borrow from the adjoining landscape. This was a reaction to the wholly enclosed formal style that had previously dominated garden making. "Leaping the fence" reminds us of the importance of linking the garden to its frame, of exploring its relationship with its surroundings.

The Italian Renaissance garden was, by contrast, a structured composition. Paintings such as the series of lunettes of the Medici villas by Giusto Utens show geometric arrangements organized around a villa or palazzo. His 1599 record of the newly finished grounds of the Villa Pratolino, just north of Florence, shows a garden designed in three areas with the landscape rigorously controlled. But it was not without humour – this garden was famous for its grottoes and water features. The great 16th-century

Above:
Painted by Giusto Utens, this 1599 lunette of the newly finished parks of the Villa Pratolino exemplifies the Renaissance ideal of a garden designed in three areas. Between the controlled planting that surrounded the villa and the forest on the scheme's perimeter, was a middle territory, a cultivated wilderness where design and Nature met.

French essayist Montaigne wrote of it that when you sit on a bench to admire the sculpture, "by a single movement the whole grotto is filled with water, and all the seats squirt water."

These Italian paintings demonstrate the three phases of the designed garden. The area close to the house was precisely organized and executed in minute detail, whereas the area outside the garden perimeter remained as forest. But then there was a middle territory, a cultivated wilderness where design and Nature met. Here routes and paths were cut through dense plantations, and clearings were made for gatherings and contemplation. Hovering between Nature and nurture, this quasi-wilderness is a doubly special place for us today: from design theory down to cultivation practices, so many of the questions that we now face when making gardens involve the extent to which we are prepared to give Nature a free hand.

Something very interesting should happen where a building meets the land surrounding it. Here we find an opportunity to explore ambiguity in design. Where does the building actually stop? Is it really at the walls or door, or is there not, in fact, an area of outside ground so warmly embraced by the architecture that it belongs both to house and garden? Even where the

Above:
Mies van der Rohe's pavilion for the 1929 Barcelona Exhibition has freestanding interior walls that never meet. As a result, its spaces flow one to another and are implied rather than enclosed. He applied the same principle to this pool, only partly wrapping it with travertine walls and leaving it otherwise open to the landscape. Belonging neither to the architecture of the pavilion nor to the landscape, the pool creates its own zone. Many exciting modern gardens exist in this ambiguous state – not quite landscape yet not wholly built.

Above:
The buildings of Le Corbusier were imbued with a rigorous geometry. Yet, as we see from this carved relief on a Marseille apartment block, the arch-Modernist designed non-structural elements in irregular shapes. Their curved forms were inspired by his proportioning system, Le Modulor, that was based on the human form. This example from modern architecture serves equally for modern gardens: organic forms coexist with, and greatly enhance, geometric outlines and structures.

landscape comes right up to the building, I still feel there is an opportunity for a zone with no roof or walls but where the details of the architecture somehow adopt the outside space. In function this area is equivalent to a European city square, and that analogy also provides inspiration for how it should be designed. It is a place that will be used for entertaining, for conversation, and as a plinth for the architecture of the house. Setting the pattern for the rest of the garden, this is where generosity of space and ideas is required.

The most important quality it can possess is a dual sense of place and enclosure. In Rome's hilltop Piazza del Campidoglio (see p.18), Michelangelo achieved both with a brilliant geometrical design that links three buildings and a stepped approach from below. The details of the piazza enter the buildings themselves through colonnades. This is a classical arrangement but one full of hierarchy and movement. In Mies van der Rohe's Modernist German Pavilion for the 1929 Barcelona Exhibition (see p.19), the interior walls are freestanding, never meeting each other, so that the spaces can flow from one to another. Spaces are implied rather than enclosed. Beyond the roof is a pool, reflective, wrapped only partly by travertine walls; elsewhere it is completely open to the landscape. It belongs neither to the architecture nor to the landscape but exists in its own zone.

The architectural or designed approach need not exclude forms that are organic, irregular, or asymmetric. Gardens give an opportunity to express the curves of hills, valleys, and rivers within a landscape. The work of the Modernist architect Le Corbusier was imbued with a rigorous underlying geometry. He was strict in his use of proportion derived from the architecture of Antiquity. Indeed, so obsessed was he with this idea that he invented his own proportioning system, Le Modulor, an adaptation of the Golden Section (see p.32) but also tied to the human form. His ideal "man" was 1.75m (6ft) tall, a figure he adopted after noting that the heroes in movies were always 6ft tall.

This is a reminder of the link that design must have to the human scale. In his architecture, Le Corbusier designed those elements of his buildings which were not integral to the structure in irregular shapes to demonstrate their freedom from the rectilinear discipline of the building itself. Their curved forms were inspired by his proportioning system and by his own work as an artist in sculptural reliefs and murals. Painters such as his contemporaries Joan Miró and Henri Matisse also worked with abstractions of the human form. Their work, among others, inspired the Brazilian landscape architect Roberto Burle Marx in his compositions for

Left and below: Although best known as a landscaper, the Brazilian Burle Marx was equally a horticulturist, painter, and sculptor. All of these interests converged in his designs for schemes such as the Odette Monteiro Garden near Rio de Janeiro (left). Many of the plants in the garden are native to Brazil and were collected by Burle Marx himself. Meanwhile, his plans (below) reveal a painterly attitude to design and the strong influence of artists such as Matisse and Miró. This polymath approach is characteristic of great modern garden makers.

gardens and landscapes. He treated private gardens, such as the Odette Monteiro Garden (see p.21), near Petropolis (which he designed in 1948 and restored later in 1988), and public landscapes as paintings in which the earth was his canvas. He was also influenced by the tropical flora of his native Brazil, which he studied, collected, and cultivated. Burle Marx deployed the smaller of these plants in vast sweeps of ground cover to block in areas of his garden "painting". Others, such as slim-trunked tropical trees and spiny succulents, he chose for their graphic qualities, their strong shapes and lines, which furnished his painting with drama. Others again, perhaps an orchid, bromeliad or heliconia, were chosen to provide brilliant highlights that would lift the entire composition.

Roberto Burle Marx and Le Corbusier were both artists, painters in spirit who chose to work in other media. Gardens are an ideal medium for artistic expression, connecting uniquely with the five senses of touch, taste, smell, sight, and sound. Artists continue to make interventions in the landscape that give us new perspectives on Nature and garden, wild and cultivated. For example, Richard Long's *Brittany Red Stone Circle* (see pp.8–9)

Below:
Ben Nicholson's artworks exhibit exactly the qualities that are the essence of the modern garden – coolly controlled colour contrasts, carefully balanced rectilinear outlines, an uncluttered, minimalist approach to space. This painting from 1937 could easily furnish inspiration for a garden layout, in which the painted forms are reinterpreted as a series of terraces – one block grass, perhaps, one stone, one water, one planting.

Right:
Despite the controversy that dogged Carl Andre's 1966 sculpture, *Equivalent VIII,* its effect is one of mesmerizing calm. It achieves this through the cool and primitive qualities of its materials, the rhythmic repetition of their grid arrangement, and a commitment to simplicity – all key factors in making modern gardens. In a world where we are bombarded by images and messages of staggering intensity and diversity, these bricks remind us how rarely it is that we encounter something so elemental, something that gives us room for our own thoughts.

combines geometry with a random mix of stone. Its pure form and rough texture not only captivate us, making us focus on a woodland scene, but they also make us question our relationship with it: would we be so aware of the wildness of this space were a human artefact not at its centre?

In making and designing new gardens we need to be in tune with other cultural activities – art, architecture, music, literature. New ideas often run in parallel, but take different forms in different media. I have taken inspiration from developments that modern art has undergone over the past century or so. Ever since Paul Cézanne, painters have re-examined the relationship of a three-dimensional subject to the flat canvas. They have sought not to conceal the image's flatness but to show the process of its translation into two dimensions through interpretation and abstraction. There is a link from Cézanne's paintings of the peak

Above:
Dan Flavin's sculpture uses the idea of the frame, made of light, to inform and transform space. We see the same space quite literally in a new light. There is separation and repetition, the ordinary and the extraordinary, all defined by a grid of light. Visiting an exhibition of Flavin's work, I was struck by the way the light source changed the colour of the landscape seen through the windows of the gallery. The familiar was now not so familiar at all.

of Mont Sainte-Victoire, near his home town of Aix-en-Provence, through the Cubist works of Picasso and Braque to Matisse and on to Richard Paul Lohse, the works becoming more abstract at each step. Gardens, likewise, are amenable to this process of abstraction, of exploring essential forms and spatial relationships.

The later paintings and reliefs of British artist Ben Nicholson are compositions reduced to the essence of the subject and almost architectural in form (see p.22). On one level they can be seen as coolly rational design compositions; on the other hand, they are conceived by an artist who is making an emotional statement through his work. Nicholson's compositions contain a hierarchy. One area of a painting appears more important than others, a focus or the centre of gravity. While squares are static, rectangles become directional. A circle or line evokes other thoughts. Colours give rectangles depth or height, but they are also flattened on the canvas. There is a celebration of the way in which one area meets another, of the use of proportion, and the balance of movement and calm.

Modern gardens can celebrate space, proportion, the contrast between areas of colourful content and cool calm, in much the same way as a painting by Nicholson. Other, more recent artists offer us lessons too. Carl Andre's 1966 sculpture, *Equivalent VIII* (see p.23), caused controversy when it was acquired by the Tate Gallery in 1972. Yet surely serenity rather than outrage is the message of this sculpture? We ponder the way in which these 120 firebricks were selected and arranged in a grid. We observe the rhythm of their repetition. These bricks demonstrate the ambiguity of simplicity, the sheer range of profound and complex speculation

Below:
Modern art is rich in lessons for garden makers. This painting by Richard Paul Lohse (*Fifteen systematic colour scales merging vertically* 1950/67) shows how it is possible to juxtapose contrasting rectangles directly within a grid of colour. These areas, tones, and rhythms would readily translate into borders, paths, and lawns.

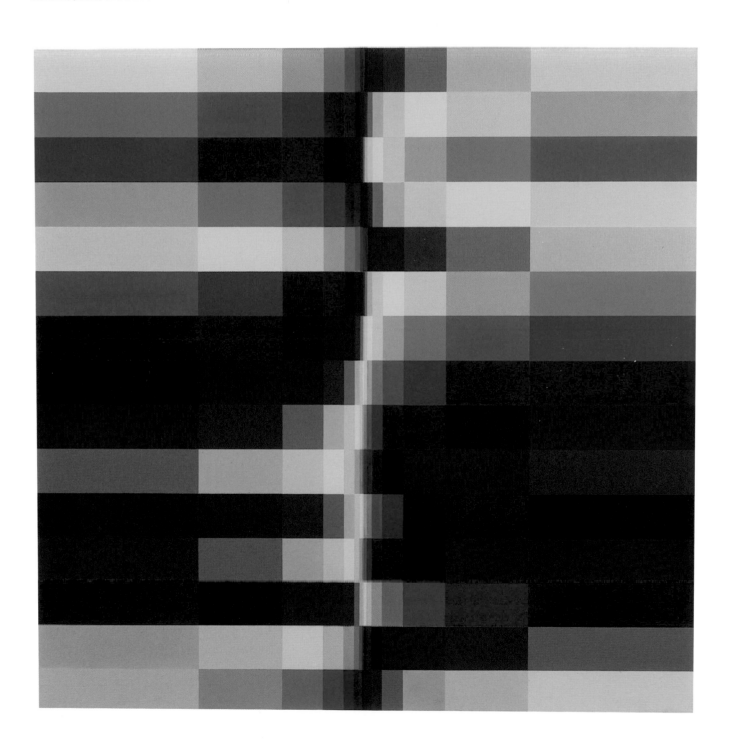

Above:
Designed by Sir Geoffrey
Jellicoe, the Kennedy Memorial
at Runnymede shows how
landscape can be both moving
and rich in meaning. On an
ascending path that winds
through woodland, each step
represents a year of Kennedy's
life; each granite cobblestone
the random pace of a pilgrim.
The summit is crowned with
a memorial stone bearing a
dedication. A straight path
alongside it points the way
to a better future.

that can be provoked by the plainest-seeming arrangements and objects. In 1961, another minimalist sculptor Dan Flavin started to work with materials that are even more common and elemental than bricks – light and space. Deploying tubular lighting to create square frames and other geometric structures (see p.24), Flavin's "architecture of light" returns us to two of the main issues in garden making: the framework and its surrounds, and the interaction of light and colour with shade and neutrality. Both these artists are also in the business of defamiliarizing the familiar, of making us reassess the commonplace and everyday. This, too, is one of the main aims of modern gardens in which we revisit one of the oldest art forms, whether using sophisticated materials like Flavin or the most basic components like Andre's bricks, and see it with new eyes.

Lighting is just one medium which interests artists and garden makers alike; gardens and lighting are natural companions. But garden making is not all about the latest techniques. It is the most timeless of the arts, containing past, present and future. It embraces life and artifice and requires us to work with that most demanding medium of all, Nature herself, to make a statement about our lives and our relationship with the planet. The state of our gardens says a lot about the state of the world. They have the power to move us. The assassination of President Kennedy in 1963 shocked the world. At Runnymede, where Magna Carta was signed in 1215, an acre of English ground was given to the American people for a memorial landscape. Steeped in Jungian thinking, landscape architect Sir Geoffrey Jellicoe used the metaphor of the pilgrimage through life to design a unique garden of remembrance. This physical interpretation of a celebrated life in the form of a modern landscape is a powerfully moving experience.

Recently, I was asked to design a garden in Weimar, Germany, inspired by plant hunting in the South Seas. This three-dimensional event is also an expression of imagination about travel, sea, vastness, wildness, dryness, and unknown terrain. The garden is divided into two areas: one, surrounded by water, contains plants of the southern hemisphere, and the other, plants of the northern hemisphere. The garden celebrates Linnaean taxonomy and plant collection, and the poet Goethe's work in developmental biology. It is also a contemporary interpretation of the impact of historical events that continue to shape our world.

Gardens, then, can be so much more than merely pleasing assemblages of form and colour. Like any other artwork, they can contain a multiplicity of meanings. In the 18th century it was customary to imbue them with meaning at every turn and, as in a great novel or symphony, this needed time and teasing out. Today, however, when gardens and other sources of gratification are expected to be easy and instant, we stand in danger of forgetting the narrative in our garden making. A thing of immense potency and plurality, the garden has fascinated writers, philosophers, artists, and patrons. But only by resonating with meaning, with ideas old and new, can it continue to be the greatest art form.

Above and below:
With the artist Insa Winkler I designed this garden in Weimar (above), inspired by the theme of plant hunting in the South Seas. Bamboo encloses a plot that is a three-dimensional meditation on travel, vastness, and unknown terrain. The design illustrates how a garden can relate a complex narrative: here, a celebration of Linnaean taxonomy, the poet Goethe's work in developmental biology, and, in two discrete areas, the plants of the southern and northern hemispheres.

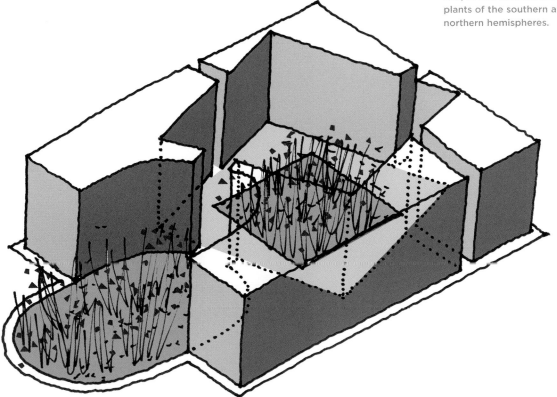

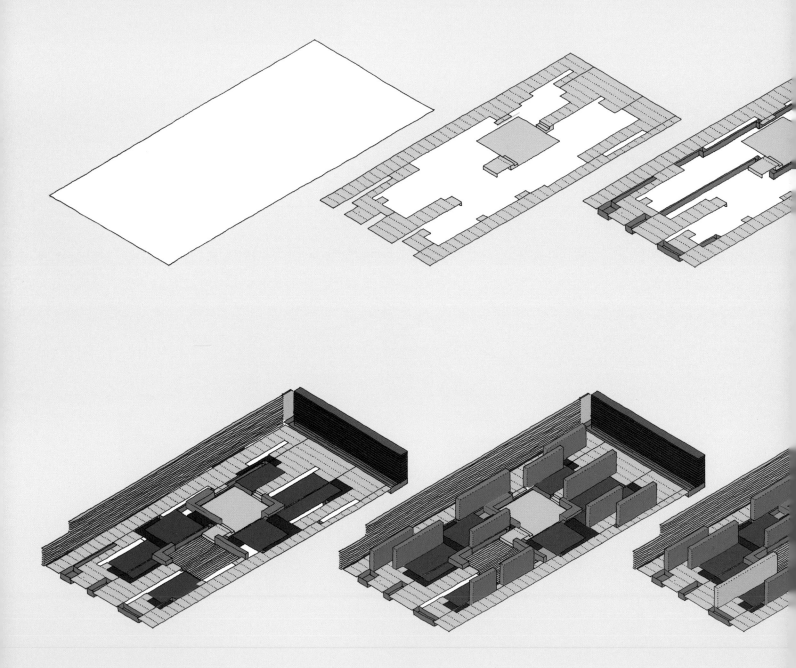

The plans for my 2004 Chelsea Flower
Show garden reveal how I use a grid.

THE GRAMMAR

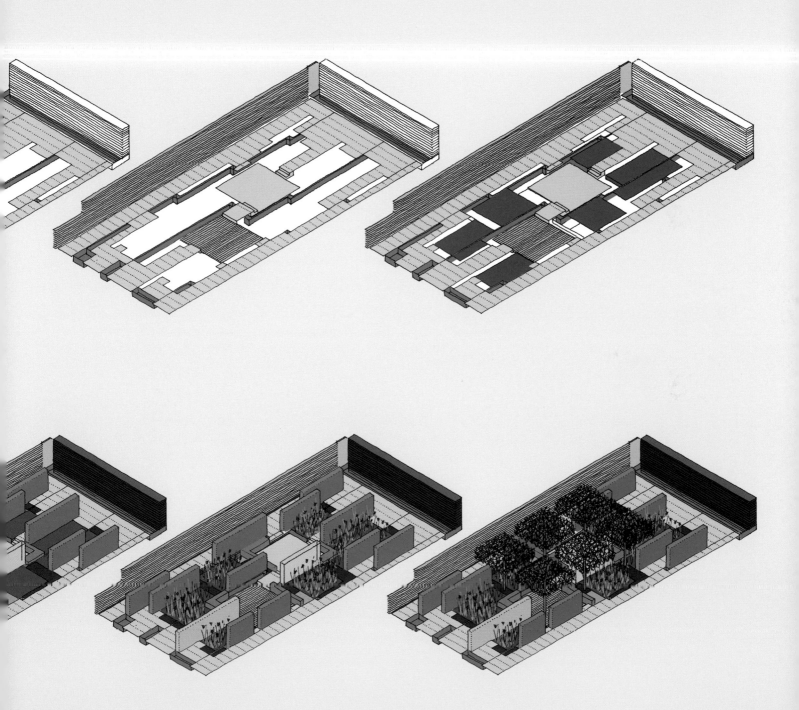

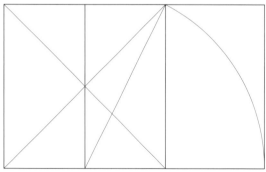

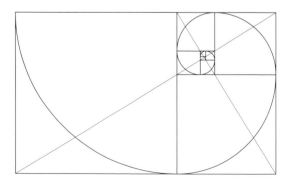

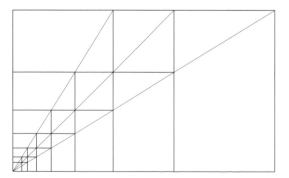

If the poetry of modern garden making lies in its inspiration and multi-layered meanings, then its basic grammar consists in the techniques and materials of design. These are the fundamentals by which a garden is composed and constructed. Modern gardens are defined by their organization and construction details. Such details must, of course, be fit for their purpose, but this entails more than just technique. Every decision regarding layout and construction has an impact on the design. Every detail, each material, and the way that they meet one other, presents a design opportunity.

A garden is explained by its form. This is the way that the various elements are grouped in relation to one another. Of all the decisions that one takes when designing a garden, the most critical is the choice of its proportions. Visitors to a garden are unlikely to say how much they admire its proportions; but I have heard them say that the garden "feels right", which amounts to the same thing.

Although the modern garden is by definition a contemporary idiom, I cannot over-emphasize the importance of understanding the philosophy of historical design ideas. This is to know your roots. Classical architecture and Modernism have fundamentally different philosophies, but many of the proportions adopted in the architecture of Antiquity have also been embraced by Modernists. To the ancient Greeks and Romans the classical "orders" were the essence of beauty and harmony. In his *Ten Books on Architecture*, the 1st century BC Roman architect and engineer Vitruvius argued that every detail should be in a fixed relationship to all others on a building, emanating from the starting point – the diameter of a column. While the dimensions could be scaled up or down to suit the size of a building, the elements had always to be in harmonious proportion to one another.

The ideas of Vitruvius were themselves rooted in the Greek world. Pythagoras, for example, expressed the Greek musical system as a numerical progression – 1:2:3:4 and by their ratios

Above and left:
Although Classicism and Modernism share fundamental design principles, their philosophies differ. Classical structures have a static grandeur, while Modernist structures are dynamic and free. Le Corbusier's Modernist Villa Stein, at Garches in France (above), has a horizontal emphasis and an asymmetrical elevation. By contrast, the Classical Palazzo Farnese, in Rome (left), is more vertical and symmetrical. The Palazzo was designed to create an air of authority, while the Villa was conceived as a dwelling machine with which one could engage and interact.

Above:
"To find beauty in form instead of making it depend on ornament is the goal to which humanity is aspiring," wrote the English landscape architect Christopher Tunnard. Around the time he published his seminal book *Gardens in the Modern Landscape*, in 1938, he completed this design at Bentley Wood in Sussex. It demonstrates the Modernist use of pure and unadorned proportion and progression in creating a series of offset or dynamic spaces. These produce an effect of visual movement, the sense that areas flow from one to another rather than remain static and unrelated.

1:2, 1:3, 2:3, and 3:4. Plato, adopting these numbers as the basis for the aesthetics of proportion, used the square and cube to produce new progressions – 1:2:4:8 and 1:3:9:27. For him these ratios were not only musical scales but also the harmony of the universe. As these Classical concepts were revived in the Renaissance, architecture came to be seen as mathematics translated into spatial units, the numerical harmonies of music and the universe in three-dimensional form.

One proportion used since Classical times is the Golden Section. It can be defined as a line segment that is divided so that the ratio of the lesser portion to the greater is the same as the greater to the whole. This proportioning system runs as a common thread from the architecture of Antiquity, through the Renaissance to the present day, where it remains a keystone of Modernism.

Although Classicism and Modernism share design fundamentals, they have diametrically opposed philosophies. Compare, for example, the Modernist Villa Stein, at Garches in France, designed by Le Corbusier in 1927, with the Renaissance Palazzo Farnese in Rome, designed by Antonio da Sangallo the Younger in 1517 and modified by Michelangelo (see p.31). While both buildings exhibit similar regulating lines and proportions in their façades, they have very different forms: the Villa Stein has a horizontal emphasis and asymmetrical elevation, whereas the Palazzo Farnese is symmetrical and more vertical. These buildings were also serving two different purposes: the Palazzo was designed to be imposing, to exude an air of authority; Le Corbusier's Villa, by contrast, was intended to be a machine for living in.

The Modernist movement has been important as an inspiration for creating modern gardens. Whereas a Classical arrangement is symmetrical, related to one centre line, and essentially static, a Modernist composition is usually asymmetrical, with a feeling of movement and dynamism. Whereas the Classical design is formal and centred on axis, the Modernist approach permits a series of experiences. Space is freed from structure and light is allowed to flood in. This approach has enabled garden-makers in the 20th and 21st centuries to create designs that are more tailored to the needs of people than were the formal set pieces of the Classical and Renaissance periods.

The contrast between the ways in which Classicism and Modernism use the vista is also revealing. In the Classical style, a vista would often be set around the centre line of a scheme, finishing on an object such as a piece of sculpture. In a Modernist

Below:
Although a Modernist, the Dutch landscape architect Mien Ruys (1904–1999) brought a highly experimental and idiosyncratic approach to garden making. The daughter of the owner of the celebrated Royal Moerheim Nurseries, she made free use of planting to structure her designs. Here she deploys a variety of hedges of different heights. These create a series of views that change as one moves around the garden.

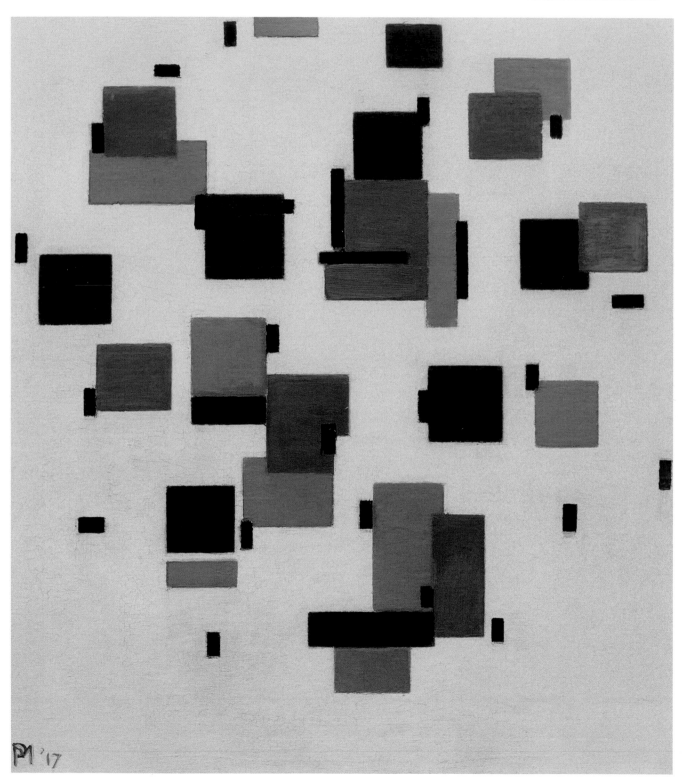

composition, where the designer is looking for movement and flowing spaces, vistas would be set to one side, encouraging the eye to look farther and to a wider view.

For garden designers, fine art goes beyond supplying inspiration and provoking thought. Paintings can also yield practical clues as to the construction of a garden composition. When we analyse some artworks, we discover a preoccupation on the artist's part with proportion and space. In Mondrian's abstract painting (left), which could be mistaken for a series of arbitrary lines painted on canvas, this sense of space is produced by a strong, underlying geometry that would be a good starting point for planning an external, or garden, space. It is not difficult to imagine some of those painted squares or rectangles as hedges, terraces, or walls, and the spaces in between them as lawn or water.

In a similar way, when one looks at the painting by Piero della Francesca (above), it is immediately apparent that the ground plan is precisely structured. The spaces are interlocking, yet they have contrasting moods. There is the rather formal composition of a piazza, but, offset to the left, there is a sense of one space

Above:
In Piero della Francesca's *The Flagellation of Christ* (c.1460), we find a sense of space which, although strictly Classical, anticipates the geometry of Modernism and offers inspiration for modern garden "rooms". Within a highly structured ground plane, interlocking spaces each have different atmospheres. Offset to the left of the formal piazza, there is one space that runs through and connects with other spaces farther on. We tend to think of spaces as being defined by the buildings that enclose them. Here, however, the ground plane, the grid of paving, alone defines and structures a space that is open to the sky.

running through and connecting with other spaces farther on. We are used to spaces being defined by the buildings that enclose them, but here we cannot fail to be aware of the importance of the ground plane and of the way it is used to structure a space that is open to the sky. Strongly architectural, Piero della Francesca's paintings demonstrate the way that a structured ground plane can be made to inform a designed landscape.

One of the greatest qualities a garden can imbue is a sense of calm. In a modern garden, this can be achieved not only by the way that spaces are formed but also by the choice of materials and the way that they are designed to meet one another. Whether the design is based on a strong, rectilinear geometry or an organic composition, there will be a feeling of calm if the design details are resolved successfully. To achieve this success, it is vital to understand and to work with the materials at your disposal. This

Below:
In this London garden that I designed, the plan is based on the Golden Section with the ground plane of a lawn as the pivot of the space. It illustrates the importance of working in proportion to the module. All the construction materials relate proportionately to its basic building block, the brick. The result is a rectilinear composition that also has a sense of great harmony.

means taking account of the size of the component materials and working to a grid that suits their modules – their basic design units. For this garden in London (left), I based the design on the Golden Section, with the ground plane of a lawn as the pivot of the space. This was a space within a space, enclosed by low brick walls with steps on one side and a wall beyond. I wanted to ensure that all the details were well considered and resolved. A brick is a standard module, so the size of the joints, steps, and wall all had to relate to the brick's dimensions, to ensure that no cutting was required. In other words, all the construction materials of the garden related proportionately to its building block, the brick. The result was a rectilinear composition that also had a great feeling of tranquility.

The garden at the Centre for Global Dialogue, at Rüschlikon in Switzerland, designed by the office of the late Swiss landscape architect Dieter Kienast, combines geometrical hard landscaping with organic planting. It reads like a delta, in which the river, that had been strongly flowing, becomes less directional as it slows down, easing itself out into the surrounding land. Despite appearances, this garden has been rigorously worked out and the planting, too,

Above:
Despite appearances, the garden at the Centre for Global Dialogue, at Rüschlikon in Switzerland, designed by the Swiss landscape architect Dieter Kienast (1945-1998), has a strong underlying geometry. Without the rectilinear rigour and empty spaces of the hard surfaces, the sinuous asymmetry of the planting would lose all definition. "We do not have to produce chaos," Kienast once remarked, "because it emerges on its own. The exterior space, however, must be a sensual place." To achieve that sensuality, he combined a variety of materials, looks, and disciplines in a highly individual and catholic approach.

Above:
At the Necco Garden in Cambridge, Massachusetts, American landscape architects Peter Walker and Martha Schwartz show how the introduction of grids to a design can energize it rather than render it static. Here, one grid overlays another in an offset, slightly rotated, pattern that engenders great dynamism. This central court, composed of two very literal and visible grids, is itself an intervention in a wider grid of tree and parkland.

has an underlying geometry. In the best artistic and design compositions, this type of deep organizing structure or pattern is invariably present even when the works themselves appear, at first, to be arbitrary.

Although it is often said that working with a grid can stultify a design, making it rather stiff and unmoving, I believe that the more rigorous the grid, the more opportunities it offers for design ideas. For example, in the context of soft landscape, a grove of trees will establish a new scale and relationship with the human form and adjacent buildings. There is great value in the regular repetition of these trees – their grid – in creating a rhythm for the design and in bringing reassurance to those who use it. Meanwhile, a grid of hard landscape will immediately define an area, putting a frame around an unstructured space.

The architecture that surrounds a site may offer a clue to the grid it requires. The proportions of windows or buildings may be reflected in the composition of the garden to create a subliminal but powerful link. Of course, there may be a variety of prevailing dimensions suggesting a confusion of grids, but this brings with it new opportunities. In my work, I often look for ways of having different grids meet and there are many design ideas that can spring from this. For example, there might be trees arranged on a 4.5m (15ft) grid relating to paving arranged on a 3m (10ft) module: ie a basic geometric pattern of 3m- (10ft-) long paved areas on which is superimposed a pattern of trees planted 4.5m (15ft) apart. The trees are thus offset from the paving pattern creating different and continually changing experiences throughout the space.

The choice of grid will impact on the nature of the space. A neutral grid with the same dimensions running in both directions, as in a square or piazza, will suggest order, a feeling of calm and a sense of place and arrival. Compare this to a straight road which subconsciously pulls us, encouraging us to travel along it. In this way a grid can help to point out, and to accentuate, the grain of the site, the direction of the design. It is important not to underestimate the value of the "ordinary", because this establishes a feeling of rhythm and repetition and a sense of safety or security. Without this given, there is no point of reference from which to spring elements of surprise. When designing in this way, it is good to start by rationalizing the plan, and then to look for the reasons to deviate from this basis and highlight the things that will make a difference in the design.

Another way of introducing a new dynamic into the design is by working with a series of grids, one overlaid on another, in an offset pattern, but also rotated. The different grids may reflect opposing geometries outside the site, or suggest routes through the site. A rigid plan can be enlivened by elements appearing off-grid

Below:
As in music and poetry, it is the self-imposed rules in garden design that make the exceptions meaningful or pleasurable. Without them, anarchy prevails. Peter Walker's landscape design at IBM Clear Lake in Texas illustrates one of the grid's most valuable properties: it is, in effect, a set of rules, a regularized pattern from which the designer is at liberty to deviate with great results. Here, a rigid plan is enlivened by trees planted off-grid or even intruding upon it: the grid is only the basis of the design and not a restriction upon it.

Above:
In the grounds of London's Tate Britain art gallery, British architects Allies and Morrison created a transcendentally simple yet technically complex landscape that comprises a series of interconnecting levels, each with its own signature materials and role. In abstract form, this design echoes and expresses the overall archaeology of the site, from the built and cultivated upper strata to the subsoil beneath them. The pleasure afforded by the progression from layer to layer, from turf to gravel to paving, illustrates the importance of creating a separation between different materials, of establishing hierarchy within design.

and not where they are expected to be. Trees or planting can be designed to intrude into the overall pattern, so demonstrating that the grid is only the basis of the design and not a restriction upon it.

As well as looking at forms and spaces when designing gardens, it is essential to consider how to work with different levels in the groundscape. Resolving changing levels satisfactorily is one of the biggest challenges for a landscape designer. There may be a choice between making the changes in level almost imperceptible, for example by working with the contours and hiding built features within a rolling landscape, and the alternative strategy of dramatizing the gradients to articulate the landscape.

Changes of level present design opportunities – for example a series of planted terraces can be repeated to create a stunning contrast with a hilly landscape. Even on the flatter parts of a site there will be levels to resolve in the way that terraces are drained. Too gentle a slope than is appropriate for the paving materials and construction quality will result in unsightly puddling; but the safer alternative of a steeper fall on the slope will also look unsatisfactory if it appears too pronounced to the naked eye. Where paving falls in two directions it can result in ugly diagonal cuts in the slabs, and unsatisfactory selection and placing of drainage grilles will make a prominent and undesirable feature.

Instead of regarding changes in level as a problem, however, it may be better to accentuate and to use them to create a new design experience. Even when starting with a completely flat space, devising different levels can prompt a highly original design, because each level can be seen as a different ground plane.

In making a garden in the grounds of the Tate Britain art gallery in London, architects Allies and Morrison created a complex landscape by expressing a series of interconnecting levels. An area of lawn, for example, is made to appear to float over an adjacent stretch of stone paving while an intermediate, recessed band of stone chippings on a lower level represents the ground layer. This design idea engages us also because it is an explanation of the archaeology of the site and so reveals much more than a single-level, fully paved area could.

I worked on a similar multi-level concept in a garden for the *Festival International de Jardins,* at Métis in Canada. Here, I created a garden that can be read through its various planes. The strongly geometric plan is accessed from both ends of the site. There is a datum plane at the general walking level and a lower plane, which includes seating areas. There are raised areas for benches and water, and another level for planting. Visitors can walk through the garden, experiencing the different levels as they move around. In the sunlight, there is a fascination in the way the differences between these levels are enhanced by shadows.

Thinking of levels is a good starting point when considering how to put together a garden design. In the plans for the garden I designed for the 2004 Chelsea Flower Show (see pp.28–29), the different levels show a progression as they build up – from the

Below:
In a garden I designed for the *Festival International de Jardins,* at Métis in Canada, I applied the concept of multiple levels in a strongly geometric plan.

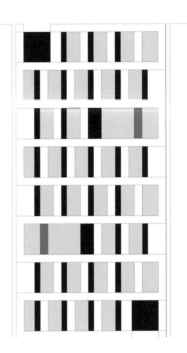

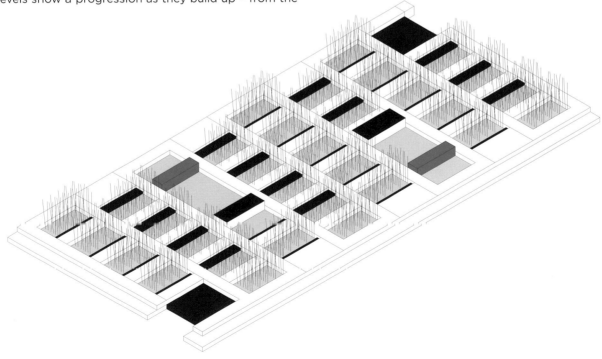

Below:
In creating this marine walk at St Valéry en Caux in Normandy, the renowned French landscape architect, Jacques Coulon explored the Modernist design principles of multiple levels and hierarchy to the full. Straight lines appear to converge and to close off access in a series of dazzling optical illusions that seem, momentarily, to thwart the very idea of promenading in any one direction. Meanwhile, the scheme's many levels and planes generate a space that is at once a pleasure ground and something far more portentous – an echo, perhaps, of battlements or the remains of ancient temples.

base plan to the paving, water, benches, hedges, trees and planting, and walls. Each of these is articulated as a separate element, occurring at a different level within the overall composition.

There are design issues particular to a large garden or landscape. Whereas intensity of detail can be maintained throughout a small garden, this may not be possible, or indeed desirable, within a large landscape. That might be partly because the cost of construction over a wide area is prohibitively expensive; but there is also the matter of whether it would be appropriate to apply the same level of detail throughout. This raises the question of the importance of hierarchy in the design.

One approach could be to make the design most intense where it is closest to the house or other buildings and to let it become progressively relaxed the farther it is from the centre of gravity. There may be intermittent highs and lows as one area changes to another, but overall there is a clear progression. This can provoke a satisfying code of details in the design. Materials might change from, say, finely clipped plants set in sawn stone near the house to wild planting separated by mown grass paths

Right:
By introducing a frame into this landscape at Issoudun, Cher, French designers Michel Desvigne and Christine Dalnoky have effected a dramatic transformation. As with a painting, the space within the frame becomes a focus of lingering attention, even when the image it surrounds, as here, is one of great directness and simplicity. Outside the frame and the pattern it contains of diverging crop lines, we find another design motif drawn from agricultural practice: a series of parallel plantations which are themselves framed. The design enacts the transformation of landscape from wilderness to cultivation, or vice versa.

in remoter areas. But what should the strategy be if the design is not directly connected to buildings, but, instead, is set within a wider and undefined landscape? In this context there will not be such a clear starting point or subsequent progression in the design. For the designer there is less to latch on to in the way of built forms. On such sites, the frame is an important device for setting a new context for a design. By introducing a frame into the landscape, the areas inside and outside it are immediately transformed. We now find ourselves looking at the site in a new way. The space within the frame becomes more special or precious and is the focus of attention. It is no longer inappropriate to treat it differently from its surroundings, and indeed we expect there to be a contrast between it and the area outside.

Now the frame will present its own design opportunities. What shape should it be? It can be rectangular like the picture frames we are accustomed to find in an art gallery. That will give one, reassuring message. But it does not have to be predictable. What about a circle, a triangle, or a rhomboid? How would these shapes affect the geometry inside and outside the frame? And should the frame be flat, raised, broken, or continuous?

Suddenly these questions become design generators, each question prompting new ideas. In its simplest form the frame will be a flat path running around the perimeter of the site. This might suit an open landscape of, say, grassland, but in a more rugged environment we may feel the need to build up the frame to create the right degree of enclosure. And do we need protection from animals or the elements? If so, we can consider framing devices other than paths, such as walls, hedges, and benches.

Now we can develop design ideas. Can there be a matrix of frames, one overlaid on another? Can they be broken in places to allow one space to flow into another? Perhaps the geometry

Above:
This car park, designed by Zaha Hadid for Hoenheim North Terminal, Strasbourg, adopts an extensive, rather than intensive, design strategy, spreading ideas thinly across a wide site. Rather than existing within a frame, elements of the design are repeated across the site at regular intervals. With the two design modules, the painted lines and the lamp posts, expressed in a harmonious sequence, the landscape becomes akin to a musical work.

within the frame can be different from that outside it, yet still reflect the geometry of a wider context? Once we imagine the frame playing the same role in a garden as it does in relation to a painting, we discover new meaning in the landscape. This method of approaching a site is more than a beginning or outline, however: it soon becomes a prompt for a range of design ideas.

A frame allows one area of landscape to be selected for special attention. But it is also a way of treating the whole landscape vicariously. The land within the frame is like a sample for approval, a fragment that enables us to imagine how the rest might look. It is a way of gardening intensively within a wide context. Alternatively, one could adopt an extensive, rather than intensive, strategy in a similar context. Instead of narrowing the focus on an isolated area, one could enlarge it by spreading design ideas thinly across a wide site. This latter approach would reveal the hidden structure of the landscape. Instead of a continuous frame, elements of the design would be repeated at regular intervals. The rhythmic lines of the landscape itself should be revealed in the way that best suits their context. At their simplest, they might be scratches in the surface, revealing, for example, the chalk underlying an area of grassland. They might be hedges, walls, or benches, or a grid of trees or a grouping of sculptural elements. They might be light fittings buried in the ground so that the rhythm of the land is only revealed at night. The important quality is repetition and the regularity of the module so that a pattern can be read.

With a rhythm established across a site there are now new opportunities to introduce design ideas that deviate from it. Here is the chance to express the unusual and to give it due emphasis: this will no longer be a modest landscape but one that has an important statement to make. It would be impossible to make that statement and to draw attention to the idiosyncratic, however, without a context of order to throw it into high contrast. There has been a trend in design to take apart rational geometries, structures, and rhythms to create an exciting new order, or deliberate disorder. In architectural schemes this form of deconstructivism may work because it rebels against the established order of street patterns, building lines and structural logic. Yet, if the normality of the background were removed, we would be left with disjointedness and chaos. That unhappy prospect demonstrates the value of the normal, the reassuring rhythms that we all need, and the importance of grammar in design.

Below:
Deconstructivism works especially well when a design is intended to express something traumatic or anarchic. The son of Holocaust survivors, Polish-born American architect Daniel Libeskind achieved exactly that impact in his building for Berlin's Jewish Museum. Created between 1989 and 1999, the museum breaks down the rectilinear integrity of built form, presenting a prospect of skewed angles, fragmentation, and subverted geometry. The result is redolent of loss, destruction, and the painful recovery of race and memory.

THE NARRATIVE

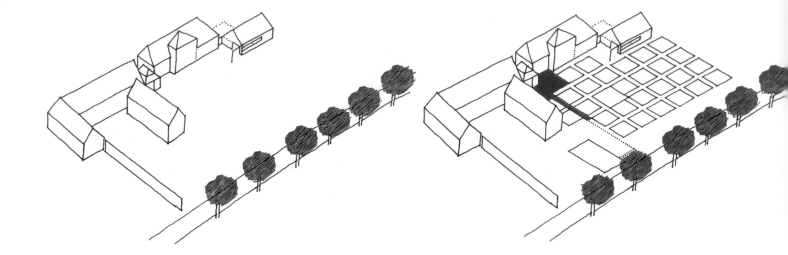

Any garden is a result of a series of questions and decisions. What to put in it? What to leave out? What style? I think of a garden in layers and consider the different elements that will be involved in creating what may become an extraordinary adventure.

A garden is physically defined by where it starts and stops. Urban spaces are likely to be confined within existing boundaries. In country gardens and landscapes we may choose to blur the edges and to borrow from the surrounding countryside. To enclose a garden or not is a fundamental decision: few other factors determine its character so comprehensively.

Enclosure will certainly influence the next decision – the form of the garden. This is the shape, the layout, the spaces and how they interrelate, their proportions and their use. One of the biggest influences will be the context of the garden. We can define context here as the sum of the prospective garden's actual site with its relationship to any nearby buildings and its position *vis-à-vis* the surrounding landscape. The garden is the middle zone between the house and its surroundings, and I like to think of the layout of the house emerging into the garden and the wider landscape also coming into this zone. What happens when these two ideas – building and landscape – meet in the garden is fascinating.

Decisions regarding form will define how, and with what, the garden makes its strongest connection. Do we want a garden that flows from the house in an almost continuous movement, emerging as a series of outside rooms? Or do we see the garden rather as an escape from everyday life, a piece of the countryside beamed in to help us forget the cares of the world?

Having decided on the degree of enclosure the new garden will have, and its relationship with its surroundings, we need next to make this new space legible to those who will enter it. We do this by adding the next layer to the design – the details. These will define the quality of the garden and the way we experience it. Details, for example, narrow our focus, creating a sense of place and a human scale even within the biggest sites. They demonstrate

Above and opposite top: If we think of elements such as a square-framed border or a rectangular hedge-cum-wall as parts of the grammar of the garden, then their assembly and cohesion could be described as its narrative. Here, in my sequence of isometric plans for the garden at Bury Court in Hampshire, England, we see that narrative unfold. The plans illustrate some of the key concepts in modern garden making – proportion, grid, frame, enclosure, rhythm, and repetition – and their imposition, layer-by-layer, on the landscape to build up a hierarchy of design.

Previous pages: A garden that I designed on the Berkshire Downs, England, is the middle zone between the house and its surroundings. The layout of the house emerges into the garden and the wider landscape also comes into this zone. What happens when buildings and landscape meet in the garden is endlessly fascinating.

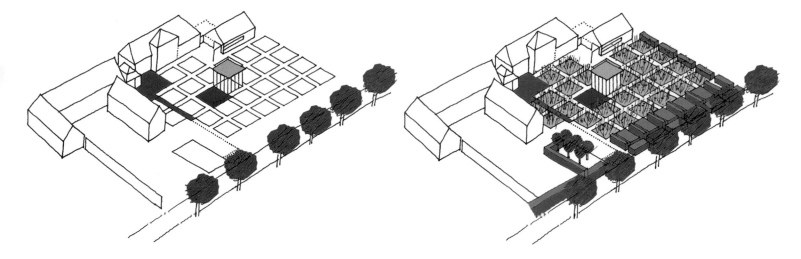

a level of attention and care that draws and holds our interest. Garden buildings, terraces, furniture, water, artworks, the use of colour, and the way that these are assembled and connected all create a narrative that gives meaning to the entire garden.

But, perhaps, the defining layer is the choice of plants and how they are used. This is where we need to be most selective because, even though gardeners today have a huge range of plants to choose from, simply adding more of them will not necessarily make our gardens interesting. On the contrary, too many plants of the wrong kind can make a garden more ordinary. The key to the choice is deciding what we want our plants to do – to add structure or colour, express the seasons, or connect with the landscape.

So, we have four layers: definition, form, detail, and planting. It is the way these layers interact that will create the character of our prospective garden. Their interaction comes down to the decisions we take – and often to what we have the courage to leave out.

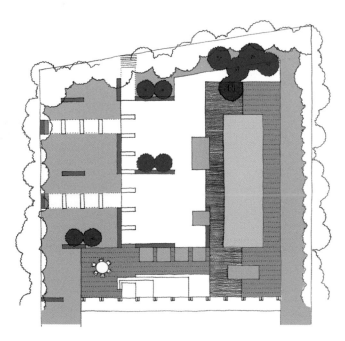

Left:
My plan for a garden at Birch Grove: garden buildings, terraces, furniture, water, art, the use of colour – the way that these are put together will create a narrative that underpins this garden.

THE ENCLOSED GARDEN

The enclosed garden has a long history – possibly the longest and most far-reaching of all garden types. Wherever civilizations have arisen, at least some of their gardens have exhibited a degree of enclosure. This was, and remains, both a matter of practical protection from the hostile environment beyond the garden and an aesthetic or spiritual issue: the garden is a place apart, a private world or sanctum in which humans are safe and sovereign.

While we can find great and ancient enclosed gardens thriving in the Far East and, in ruined form, in Classical Rome and the Pre-Columbian Americas, it is the Middle East, from Pre-Islamic times to the present, that offers many of the most significant examples of this design type. It is these that have most influenced Western attitudes to the enclosed garden today. Their immense power as artworks owes much to their location. These are desert gardens. Everything outside their walls appears desolate, barren, disordered, and subject to the harsh elements. Within the sheltering embrace of their walls, however, we find order, shade, water, and abundant planting. Here is a garden that makes life possible despite monstrous odds, and herein lies its mystique.

It is hardly surprising, then, that one Persian term for a garden, *pairidaeza*, also means "enclosed space", and that from this word we derive "Paradise" and one of the world's most important spiritual metaphors. Eden was first and foremost a walled garden. Consciously or not, garden-makers have been trying to regain it ever since the Fall. To put it another way and free ourselves from Christian imagery, the enclosed garden is civilization in microcosm, an expression of our desire to create order from chaos. It is an affirmation of life where, without our intervention, life would struggle or expire.

The Latin term *hortus conclusus*, used since medieval times, often referred to a garden within a garden that was imbued with religious and literary symbolism. "A garden inclosed is my sister, my spouse; a spring shut up, a fountain sealed," says *The Song of Solomon* in the King James Version, linking the walled gardens of the Renaissance to those of the ancient Middle East. The rectangular shape of these

Left:
Designed in the late 1960s by the late Mexican architect, Luis Barragán, the San Cristóbal Stables show one of the oldest principles of garden making – enclosure – at its most modern.

Although minimalist, this design connects closely with Nature via glimpses of the sky and the surrounding landscape, and through the sun-soaked earthy colouring of its walls.

Below and opposite:
The original purpose of
enclosing a garden was to
enforce a strong practical and
aesthetic distinction between
the cultivated space inside
the enclosure and the wild
landscape outside it. Recently,
however, garden designers
have questioned this approach.
Wilderness is, after all, often
beautiful and increasingly
precious. To maintain it, or the
appearance of it, also requires
discipline, a form of husbandry,
that is just as demanding as
conventional horticulture, if not
more so. Why not invert the
hortus conclusus concept by
enclosing wilderness instead?
In these two images of a
garden created by Teresa Gali-
Izard in Girona, Spain, we see
the untamed native landscape,
or a semblance of it, placed
within walls. The result is like
a quotation or a precious
fragment of something
beautiful and vulnerable.

gardens paralleled the form of the cloister, itself descended from domestic Roman architecture. The enclosing hedges or walls performed a functional as well as symbolic role, offering protection to the plants and their owners. Within the outer framework, these gardens were subdivided by paths into a series of similar-sized beds and areas.

The Italian *giardino segreto*, or "secret garden", was an extension of this concept. At first a small and solitary garden "room", it later became the inspiration for the Italian Renaissance garden with its multiple collection of "rooms", in which the idea of geometric composition based on exquisite proportions and elaborate detail reached its zenith.

At the very heart of these gardens, too, is the notion of order, with emphasis on clearly defined layout. Precisely clipped plant forms were used to demonstrate a sense of order within the walls of the garden, in sharp contrast to the chaotic natural disorder of the woodland beyond.

These ideas were given their own interpretation in Northern Europe where courtly Renaissance gardens were made on a grand scale. For example, the Hortus Palatinus in Heidelberg, Germany was designed by Salomon de Caus on the principle of long narrow terraces within high retaining walls. These contained gazebos, pools, a maze, statuary, plants, and spectacular waterworks and fountains. In the 20th century, the enclosed garden tradition was

developed further to encompass the idea of creating a flowing series of rooms in the garden, thereby emphasizing its connection with the house to which it was attached. When Modernist designers adopted and adapted these ideas, building on their knowledge of historical tradition and departing from strict Classical notions, the results were dynamic. Whereas Classical rules produced an essentially static effect, a Modernist approach allowed the spaces to become more fluid and instilled a greater feeling of movement. An enclosed garden relates more closely to the house than an open garden, and a Modernist treatment allows for an exploration of this relationship, generating an exciting ambiguity and interplay between what is within and what is beyond.

The Mexican architect Luis Barragán developed a series of projects which explored this interplay of fluidity and enclosure. The San Cristóbal Stables (1967–68), designed for the Egerstrom family on a site to the north of Mexico City, demonstrate the way in which walls and buildings can be used to describe a space in the landscape which is at once open and enclosed. The power of the space is emphasized, not reduced, by the containing buildings. These are designed to express their importance in the hierarchy of the design. Meanwhile, the geometry of the space is only implied by the connecting walls. Huge openings are cut from the boundary walls, encouraging views through and beyond them and reinforcing the sense of shelter and enclosure.

Simply enclosing a garden has the effect of placing it within a frame or showcase. Without changing the planting inside or outside the frame, the interior space is changed. It becomes

concentrated, separated, rarefied, distilled; it provokes fresh and intense thoughts. Suddenly the garden becomes an extension of the house, another room with a human scale. Before enclosure, the house and its surroundings are a small part of a much wider landscape. After enclosure there is a new ambiguity between house and garden. Where does the inside stop and the outside start? When the scale of the landscape is reduced to human dimensions we start to comprehend its shape and proportions in a different way. Up close, we notice the details, the way walls meet the ground, the way plants meet paving.

In warm climates, and with new construction techniques, this ambiguity is heightened; the house can be opened to the elements to allow greater connection between building and environment. We can begin to imagine the garden space as a part of the home from which the roof has been removed. The walls and finishes can be thought of in the same way as with other rooms, but here the elements can intervene; plants can grow and we can connect with the sky and the stars.

In traditional forms of the enclosed garden, the emphasis was on making a strong separation between the wilderness outside the walls and the artificial planting within. Another approach is to create a connection between the enclosed space and the area beyond by bringing in, or echoing, wild vegetation from the landscape. Here the demarcation between the two areas is far less distinct. This generates a pleasing ambiguity; it has the effect of treating the whole area as one big garden, with the walls superimposed upon it arbitrarily. In such a composition the walls become more than just a boundary: they are, in fact, a crucial element of the garden.

When, through naturalistic planting, a garden establishes a connection between the precise form of the house and the surrounding country, the building can appear to rise dramatically out of the landscape in a bold, modern reinterpretation of the relationship between the Classical house and its wild environs. It is reminiscent of Renaissance Italian villas, such as Andrea Palladio's Villa Capra, "La Rotunda", in Vicenza, northern Italy, or 18th-century, Classical English country houses. In both of these examples, the house is surrounded by parkland – often fields of long grass grazed by animals – which throws the built form into stark but satisfying relief.

In the traditional forms of enclosure, stone walls or hedges were normally used for the boundaries. Today, we can consider a variety of options. It is possible, for example, to create precise

walls from comparatively simple materials, such as render on blockwork. This makes a significant statement about the very act of enclosure, a new variation on a very old theme that both reflects and departs from long-established tradition.

A key factor in the success and readability of this approach is the purity of the composition. As the greatest Modernist designers have proved, no matter how novel your materials may be, they must retain a sense of exactitude and harmony. Walls that have clean lines and are crisply finished can be used to create a pure, sometimes astonishing, intervention. The quality of the scheme relies on the extreme precision of the walls and the elimination from them of all decorative details. This has the effect of creating a simple "box", which is enough to make the wildness it contains read clearly as a deliberate design idea.

Traditionally – in the cottage garden, for example – walls were softened by clothing them with climbing plants. This served to blur the boundary between the garden and the outside world, creating a sense of continuity with the countryside. I prefer to emphasize clarity and space within a garden and to reveal the full extent of the site. This is particularly true in densely populated urban areas, where the need to maximize garden space is paramount. Planted, or plant-clothed, boundaries also lose their ability to express shadows, the changing light being absorbed and lost in the mass of plants.

In bright conditions the quality of the sunlight creates strong contrasts. In a walled garden, these can be harnessed and emphasized, becoming a key element in the design. Here, shadows can be read most clearly on walls that are simple and pure in form. Such walls become canvases, or projection screens, on which the play of light and shade is graphically

Below:
As with other principles of modern garden design, such as the frame and grid, enclosures can be multiple, an idea that can be repeated within a single site. In this garden that I designed (below and on the previous pages), the entire site is enclosed as, too, are the terraced and planting areas within it. At each level of the design, different materials achieve the enclosure. Their harmony is ensured by a single system of proportion and by judicious repetition of details such as the ferrous finish of both the left-hand planting area and the end wall panel (coloured red in this plan).

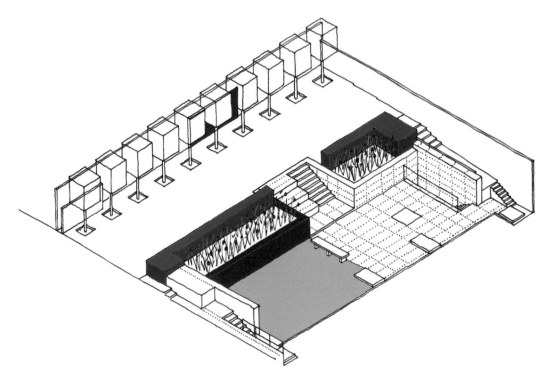

Above and left:
In a traditional enclosure, boundaries were usually constructed from hedges or stone walls. Today we can consider a wide variety of alternatives. In this garden that I designed, glass is the enclosing material. Different types of glass play with the idea of enclosure in a series of new variations on an old theme. Opaque surfaces admit only diffuse light and the darkest of silhouettes; mirrors reflect and multiply the garden's internal features; clear glass provides a window on the landscape beyond. Each type is a boundary that is solid yet permeable, while allowing a degree of visual communication with the outside world.

expressed. Walls not only serve as boundaries; they also create the opportunity to impose an individual design identity. Boundary walls can become a focal point, drawing the eye and forming an important part of the overall composition, or they may be used simply as a background.

Through the natural hues of their own materials or when painted, walls also allow us to introduce colour into the garden and to change the mood of the space. The choice of wall colour should be influenced by its ability to complement plants, and some succeed better at this than others.

Green, for example, might seem an obvious choice and is often used, mistakenly, by garden owners. In fact, it is possibly the worst colour to use in a garden because it always suffers by comparison with the green of the plants. It neither equals the beauty of the natural shades, nor fades into the background. Grey, on the other hand, is one of the best colours to use because it enhances the plant tones. Blue, which contrasts well with most flowering plants, is another good choice. I also find that earthy tones, such as yellow ochre and terra-cotta, are successful in warming the atmosphere of the garden. In sunny conditions bright colours connect with the light, but they can look incongruous under dull skies.

The two examples shown here – a roof garden in San Francisco and a garden in London – illustrate different ways in which blue panels have been used to create a boundary within a garden. In

Below:
In this garden in San Francisco designed by Topher Delaney, a series of interconnecting grey and blue panels has been used to form a Modernist composition reminiscent of the work of 20th-century painters such as Ben Nicholson. The wall reads strongly as an element in its own right, needing no additional planting to enhance it.

the London example (above), the panel stands as a refined inner layer to the boundary line and provides a backdrop for multi-stemmed *Amelanchier* trees. The soft blue-grey of the panel throws into highlight the sculptural quality of their stems, while its horizontal proportions connect with the undersides of the trees' canopies. When the trees produce their outstanding display of blossom in early summer the panel helps to create an exhilarating feeling of lightness because the white flowers seen against the blue form an abstract recreation of the sky.

In design terms, panels need to be pure in form and to accentuate either the vertical or the horizontal dimension of the garden space. This principle is developed in the San Francisco example (left), where a series of interconnecting grey and blue panels has been used to form a Modernist composition reminiscent of the work of 20th-century painters such as Ben Nicholson. Here the wall reads strongly as an element in its own right, needing no additional planting to enhance it.

Both of these designs illustrate the impact of flat colour on flat panels. Their interest is created purely by the colour, the proportions, and the interplay of different patterns.

Many gardens habitually reinforce the idea of separation from the house. Even within a town setting, the garden is conventionally seen as a type of rural retreat. To achieve this separation, the garden is laid out to emphasize the differences between itself and the house: lawns and beds are irregular in shape; paths wind; the boundaries of borders are disguised with profuse planting. Although

Above:
In this London garden that I designed, a panel provides a backdrop for multi-stemmed *Amelanchier* trees. Its soft blue-grey tone throws into highlight the sculptural quality of the trees' stems, while its horizontal proportions connect with the undersides of their canopies. In early summer the panel creates an exhilarating sense of lightness, as the white flowers seen against the blue form an abstract recreation of the sky.

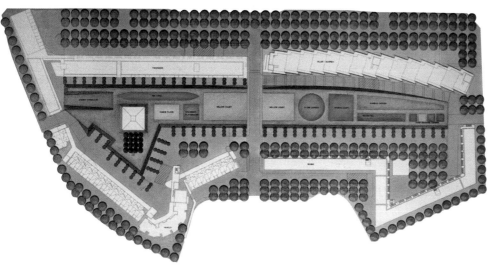

Above and left:
At the Gifu Kitagata Apartment Building in Japan, American landscape architect Martha Schwartz has created a garden that aspires to the condition of abstract modern art. Planting is reduced to a minimum or absent. Instead, what makes this place a garden is the use of modern and often brilliantly colourful materials in defining an external space as a source of pleasure and surprise. Despite delivering "the shock of the new", this garden retains the time-honoured concepts of geometric proportion, grid, and enclosure.

this strategy is adopted by many millions of gardeners, I feel it fails completely to express one of the most pleasing and exciting qualities possible in a garden – that of a seamless connection between interior and exterior, in which the house continues into the open in the form of a series of outside rooms.

One way of expressing that quality is to allow the shape of the building to emerge into the garden and to let the characteristics of the internal rooms to inform the outside spaces. In this way there is a strong connection between house and garden – the two being equal parts of a total composition. It is surprising how many clues a house can provide to the optimal design for its garden, especially if one relaxes, looks, and lets it happen.

In designing and making the garden of a London villa, which had been extensively reworked by the architects Eric Parry, this was the approach I adopted, reinterpreting the ideas of the house's internal spaces outside. The existing levels of the back garden meant that it was ideally placed to make a strong connection with the rooms that faced it. On a sloping site, the raised garden occupied an intermediate level between the ground floor of the house and a new, large, external terrace on the roof of the ground-floor extension.

My starting point was to establish a large, lawned terrace running the full width of the site on this half level, which would become the focus from the ground- and first-floor rooms. By introducing a line of retaining walls, there would be room for

Below:
When using panels, walls, and other flat-surface features in the modern garden, choice of colour is of key importance. Here, in one of the enclosures from Martha Schwartz's garden for the Gifu Kitagata Apartment Building, in Japan, we see a combination of translucent greys and blues that evokes a mood of cool or mystery. To create correspondingly altered moods, she has also used sharp yellows and glowing reds.

Left and below:
One of the great opportunities presented by modern gardens is the potential for allowing a building to emerge into a garden and to share or reflect its properties in a single artistic composition. At the Rijksmuseum Twente in the Netherlands, Dutch architect Lodewijk Baljon has created an entrance hall that sits astride a lake. The sharp and skewed outlines of the lake mirror the strong and sloping horizontals of the hall. To soften the hard lines of this dramatic union, Baljon has planted the lake with naturalistic rushes – a brilliant stroke of *rus in urbe*, the country in the town.

generous spaces flush with the ground floor and relating directly to the adjoining rooms. There was an opportunity to let the character of the internal spaces define this terrace. So here is one space, formal and precise, clad in limestone and relating to an internal gallery. Like a gallery, it is deliberately left clear. In its way untouchable, this is an abstract space, free to receive ideas and to let in natural light.

In contrast to it is the more relaxed terrace, paved in western red cedar slats, which directly relates to the kitchen and family room. This is a busy space; one to spill into, for games and relaxation, and for plants in containers. The retaining wall on the upper terrace is rendered in a Venetian polished plaster. Although the finish is warm and natural, this is a fine material no less formal than the adjoining stone.

A hallway separating the principal rooms of the house is expressed externally by a set of wide stone steps. They form the main route to the upper lawn terrace and are focused on a second rendered wall at the top of the garden, which is designed to the horizontal proportions of a double square. Over-large steps that double up as stone benches run alongside the walkway. These cut through a zone of naturalistic planting, of grasses and other upright perennials, that creates a colourful veil facing the house. A substantial yew hedge protects it from the lawned play area on the upper terrace.

Near the boundary, a line of hornbeams, sculpted to form a stilt hedge, emphasizes the width of the garden and reinforces the idea of horizontal lines and the concept of steps and terraces.

Above:
In the courtyard of the Stadhuis IJsseltein in the Netherlands, Lodewijk Baljon again takes care to marry landscape with building. Here, a rugged surface of rock, gravel, and sporadic tufted grasses is broken by a pattern of narrow rectangular pools. Of differing widths and lengths but all running east–west, these pools echo the powerful verticals of the surrounding building. Seen from above, their open configuration of broken grey lines recalls the paintings of another Dutch master, the artist Piet Mondrian.

GARDEN OF THE DESERT

Many historic gardens contained an underlying narrative and were rich in symbolism. Modern gardens are no less appropriate as vehicles for articulating complex ideas and powerful messages.

My inspiration for this garden was the desert of Abu Dhabi and the remarkable vision of its then ruler and first President of the United Arab Emirates, the late Sheikh Zayed. Through irrigation and planting schemes, the Sheikh halted the process of desertification and restored some of Arabia's most precious and beautiful ecosystems. So the garden aims to express the beauty of the true desert and its flora, but also the role that water and cultivation have played in returning desertified land to its original fertility. It is also about enclosure, separation, and progression: the experience of moving from one space to another, from exposure to shelter and from arid wilderness to oasis. In this it echoes the ancient enclosed paradise gardens of Arabia, drawing on one of the world's oldest and greatest gardening cultures.

At the pivot of the plan is a glass pavilion in the form of a cube, the molecular module of salt. It symbolizes the process of desalination, which has been fundamental to the success of planting the desert in Abu Dhabi. One of the difficulties with growing in the desert is coping with the saline conditions, but Abu Dhabi has been able to make use of its coastline to produce fresh water through desalination. In this garden, a colonnaded stone wall separates plants growing in desert conditions from those irrigated by a system of water channels and a reflecting pool.

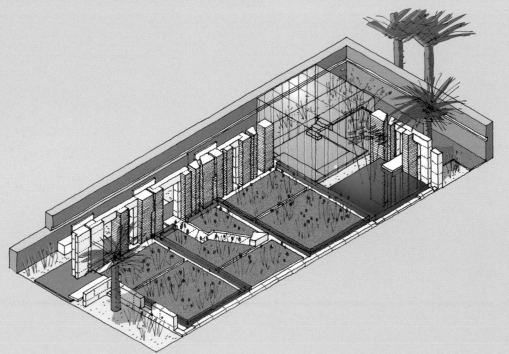

Above left:
The wall is made of hand-crafted sandstone with a smooth inner layer. A sawn-stone bench is cantilevered through an opening in the wall to hover over a reflective pool.

Left:
This layout of the garden shows the separation created by the dry-stone wall and the glass pavilion at the pivot of the plan. Areas within the wall represent beds of planting irrigated by a series of glass water channels.

Right:
A view of the "desert" area of the garden reveals a walkway of ipe wood enclosing a planting zone with trees of *Ziziphus jujuba* growing in sand. This part of the garden is bounded by the dry-stone wall, the glass pavilion, and a perimeter wall rendered with sand from Abu Dhabi.

Right:
The modern garden can contain many strands of narrative, all interwoven to convey a single powerful message or impact. In my *Garden of the Desert,* I presented the story of regeneration through irrigation. The planting, for example, replicates the flora of Arabian oases and *wadis,* an arid landscape transformed by water. The colours and textures of the stonework and sandy surfacing materials represent the desert, while the glass that contrasts with them has the shimmering transparency of water. Meanwhile, cut into the walls, are fragments of Arabic calligraphy that echo the famous words of the man who inspired this garden, the late Sheikh Zayed. When he was told that he would never be able to irrigate and regenerate the desert, the Sheikh said, quite simply, "Let's give it a try." This garden celebrates the fact that he succeeded.

Left:
This Paris apartment complex
by Italian architect Renzo
Piano demonstrates two
important morals of modern
design. The first is that,
when conceived and executed
with care and attention to
detail, Modernism can be
a remarkably human and
uplifting style – the fact
that this building is a social
housing block should stand as
a lesson to all planners. The
second moral is similar to the
first in that it involves a sense
of liberty within order: even
the most disciplined modern
landscape can be a place of
great freedom and elation.
Here, French landscapers
Michel Desvigne and Christine
Dalnoky have mirrored the
terra-cotta facing of Piano's
building in a rigidly regular
floor plane. Equally regular
are the planting areas, yet
the result is a garden that
generates an atmosphere of
liberation and wilderness.

In height, the canopies of the hornbeams relate directly to eye level on the first-floor terraces. The roof terrace is, in effect, an outside extension of the upper rooms of the house which spill on to it. This terrace is finished in a mixture of wood and stone, with areas broken up by the texture of pebbles and planting. The stone I used here is the same as that inside the house, laid precisely to create a calm, minimalist external space. The glass balustrading allows a complete, unbroken connection to the garden below, while its reflective qualities introduce a satisfying ambiguity into the two areas.

By keeping the lower terraces within the exact width of the house there are slots at each side of the garden in which two sets of secondary brick stairs can rise alongside the existing garden walls. Choice and progression are important in a design: in this garden, I have given the owners a number of choices – a new route, from formal to informal, up or down. Within one enclosure there is a series of experiences defined by position, level, materials and plants.

Creating a large landscape within a wider urban setting presents a different kind of challenge. Here, context demands a design in scale with the tall buildings that dominate the environment. The pattern of the landscape must be appropriate for the scale and the modular dimensions of the surrounding architecture. The task is to make the design part of the townscape yet, at the same time, to give it a human quality, so people can relate to the space on both an intimate and monumental level. This is a difficult balance to achieve, for the

Above:
The Paris apartment block landscape by Desvigne and Dalnoky illustrates a further important point about making modern gardens. As with painting and sculpture in Modernism, these gardens involve a process of reduction and abstraction to achieve powerful and complex effects. What we have here is, in essence, wild northern woodland, a soulful communion of sunshine-scattering canopy, graceful but graphic tree trunks, and dense understorey. Yet one could only reproduce that habitat literally and in all its true complexity with the greatest difficulty. Even then it would probably not say "woodland" but, rather, "chaos". So the modern designer distils and abstracts, recreating the spirit of Nature, in this case, with just two very durable plants – birch and evergreen honeysuckle.

SCREENS, BOUNDARIES, AND WALLS

We look to walls and fences to create the external boundary of a garden. One of the requirements may be to achieve protection and security: to make a physical barrier. Where security is not the prime concern, boundaries can still be important to announce the demarcation of a site, where it starts and ends.

It may also be important to make a walled enclosure within a garden to act as a windbreak, for the purpose of protecting vulnerable plants, or simply to create a series of "rooms" to give the viewer a sequence of separate experiences. However they are used in garden design, as protective boundaries or as visual or physical dividing elements, walls and fences provide an opportunity for artistic expression.

The design of walls – their layout, the materials chosen, and the openings within them – will do much to convey the quality and atmosphere of a garden. The spaces created by their enclosures should always read well, even before any plants are introduced. Their key characteristics are the proportions of the enclosures, the heights of the walls, the way one wall meets another, and how their openings and entrances are created. All of these factors will

Below:
I designed this English country garden with a stone wall that both encloses the site and, through a series of apertures, frames the vista beyond. Two types of stone finish combine to imbue this otherwise simple-seeming structure with an intriguing complexity: the laid, rough-faced walling is redolent of centuries (if not millennia) of craftsmanship, while the precisely sawn and perfectly finished arches speak of modernity and urbanity. Together, the two materials impart a monumental quality to this wall that is both ancient and contemporary.

Above:
The perfect material and perfect finish – in this garden in Phoenix, Arizona, the American landscape architect Steve Martino uses one of his trademark colour-washed walls to echo the palette of the surrounding desert and to act as a canvas for a gauntly sculptural boojum tree.

determine the critical experience of the garden enclosure. By their very nature, external boundaries are likely to be more extensive than internal walls and so their qualities and detail will probably have to be more thinly spread. Because they can cover a large perimeter, boundary walls and fences are also likely to encounter changes of level and direction. Here, it is advantageous if the wall or fence can be of modular form. If it can be designed as a series of elements – panels, for example – any changes of level and direction can be managed by the way in which one module meets another and yet retains its individual form regardless of situation.

Entrances in boundaries are an opportunity to express the idea of the "threshold" – the notion that the experience offered within is unlike that outside. So an entrance should be considered a point of intrigue, arresting and beckoning. Here detail should be at its most expressive and sculptural to command attention. Special thought should be given to the way the ground plane and paving materials meet the threshold. Doors or gates may be necessary for security, but may be left open in the daytime: the well-designed, open gateway can be an eye-catcher, an irresistible come-hither invitation to the viewer.

Opposite below:
Designed by Bet Figueras and Oscar Tusquets, this wall of overlapping semicircles in Girona, Spain, shows the importance of taking landscape and locale into account. Although attempting something playful and experimental, the wall remains consonant with its context through its warm terra-cotta tones. This is an excellent example of the flexibility of modular design, the modules (semicircles in this case) easily negotiating the undulating terrain.

Below:
One of the great excitements of Modernism in gardens is that it challenges fundamental ideas. Why should a wall be an impermeable barrier or screen? Might it not be given other properties? In this garden near San Francisco, Topher Delaney deconstructs the idea of the fence to create a "barrier" that admits light and landscape, is itself a striking sculpture, and, perhaps most beautiful of all, imposes a graphic design on the garden through its own slotted shadow.

garden or landscape spaces must be in proportion to the mass of the buildings around them. One solution to this issue of scale is to repeat smaller elements so that they build up into a bold pattern. This approach can allow the grid of the landscape to emulate the buildings around it without being dominated by them.

For a precursor of the principle, we should look outside the urban cityscape to early 20th-century English gardens, such as those at Sissinghurst Castle, in Kent, and Hidcote Manor, in Gloucestershire. These were designed as a series of interconnecting rooms with planted hedges or rustic stone walls defining the spaces. These rooms conferred an intimate human scale on what would otherwise have been forbiddingly large gardens

With a reinterpretation of this approach, rooms can be created within an urban context. But we are no longer confined to hedging and stone walling. Modern materials and energy sources allow us to create high-tech enclosures, rooms defined, illuminated, and even made sonorous by, for example, coloured panels, ingenious lighting, and walls of water.

These materials are especially suited in character to landscapes made within a cityscape. They allow us to inhabit and enjoy what would otherwise be a rather bleak and hostile environment. If we

Below and opposite:
Working with the vernacular, with local materials and traditions, is a well-established principle in design. Few designers have espoused it quite so imaginatively as the American Steve Martino, however, and certainly not a vernacular so uniquely specialized and local as that of the Arizona desert. In form, texture, and colour, Martino's walls echo the region's indigenous architecture. The plants that he uses are also desert natives. The result is both truly modern and entirely in harmony with the place it inhabits. It also offers lessons for garden-makers outside desert regions – purity of line; respect for *genius loci*, the spirit of the place; and sparing but judicious choice of plants.

enlist the help of new technology, we can make our garden rooms into places of comfort and intimacy by day and of romance and drama by night.

In the past, roofs of public buildings were too often regarded as wasted spaces or used to accommodate ancillary services, pipework, and air-conditioning plant. But a compelling idea has emerged of late: whenever a building development lays claim to potential landscape space at ground level, the equivalent space should be created at roof level by way of compensation.

Green spaces are vitally important, enhancing our well-being and that of the wider environment. Forward-thinking planning authorities and designers are responding to this fact by pursuing the concept of the green roof. As we continue to develop more and more of our land, why should the space taken away at ground level not be restored at the top of the building?

So the rooftops of major public buildings are becoming emblematic of increased environmental responsibility. These new roofscapes may be enjoyed from internal viewing points or seen from street level like so many giant green flags. If a roof is

Left and opposite: Modernism should not imply a rejection of time-honoured materials and techniques – not all is glass and metal, painting and lighting. The Belgian designer Jacques Wirtz is renowned for his use of plant material – hedges, topiary, and screening trees – in creating landscapes that have all the formal beauty of something done in stone or concrete, and yet are entirely alive and green.

made into a garden, that puts gardens and the importance of public green space at the forefront of our thoughts. As public/private buildings of some prestige, museums, theatres, art centres, and galleries present special opportunities for conveying this message. External spaces are a welcome contrast to the interior and can become display areas such as sculpture galleries; outside terraces make pleasant cafés and restaurants; the less accessible areas of roofs can be designed, planted, and treated as pieces of sculpture in their own right. What better place for a planting that celebrates local topography, geology, and flora than a regional museum?

The J Paul Getty Center, home to one of the world's foremost art organizations, is an imposing collection of buildings on a hilltop site in Brentwood, overlooking the city of Los Angeles, California. The Center, which opened in December 1997, was the

Below:
When we look at the work of Jacques Wirtz, as in this garden near Maarkedal, Belgium, we realize that hedging, a material so familiar and bound by convention, can be liberated, reconsidered, and reworked to create spaces of true originality and mystique.

HEDGES

The hedge has been an important element of gardens from their very beginnings. In the medieval *hortus conclusus* it was used as a marker, to define space and to bring privacy and shelter. By the early 14th century, European literature contained references to hedges made of thorn, roses, quince, nut, and plum. Pomegranate was sometimes a favoured alternative in warmer climates.

Long before then, however, the Romans used box and rosemary for outlining a design, and in the 1st century AD Columella referred to enclosure using living fences of rooted osier branches. In *The Gardeners Labyrinth* (1577), Thomas Hill refers to this use of willows and to "quickset hedge for inclosure" using whitethorn and blackthorn. But it was in writings on the Italian Renaissance gardens that the design potential of hedges was first proclaimed. In *Hypnerotomachia Poliphili* (published in English as *Poliphili's Strife of Love in a Dreame* in 1499), Francesco Colonna (1433-1527) describes a perfect garden in which there are hedges and topiary of fantastic elaboration and extravagance.

The maze first began to appear in Renaissance gardens in the 15th century and by the 17th century had become commonplace in the grander schemes. Du Cerceau (*Les Plus Excellents Bastiments de France* 1576 and 1579) refers to many mazes and features shaped from box and yew, but also hyssop, thyme, and santolina, and it was in the northern European gardens of the 17th century that the potential of hedging as a design feature was most fully explored. The gardens of Trianon, alongside Versailles, displayed straight *allées* (tree-lined avenues)

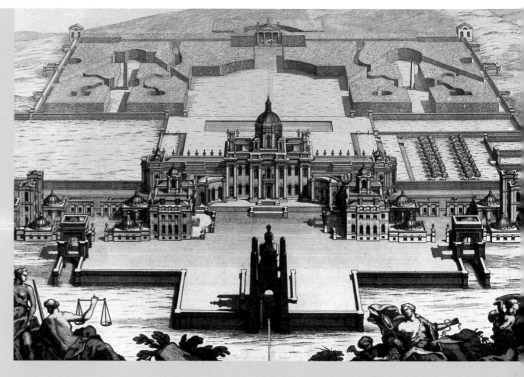

and clipped hedges on an impressive scale. This trend took root at a time when the owners of great houses could employ huge teams of gardeners to clip hedges into fine shapes – thereby demonstrating the extent of both their wealth and their ability to control the surrounding landscape. The gardens created by the great French designer André le Nôtre (1613–1700) were the ultimate expression of such power and affluence.

In England, one of the unrealized plans at Castle Howard was for a massive hedge made over a vast area in the shape and scale of a building with openings or rooms cut from it – dramatic openings to be sculpted out of what was originally a single

structure. Bramham Park, in West Yorkshire, features huge beech hedges. In other 18th-century examples, such as St Paul's Walden Bury, we see tall beech hedges used to form vistas in the style of Le Nôtre as a forerunner of the English landscape park.

In the "wilderness" at Ham House we find a complex arrangement of hornbeam hedges, interlaced with stilt forms and top knots. Composed of parallel lines of trees with their trunks bared and their crowns fused and clipped into a single rectangular mass, pleached stilt hedges were developed as a variation on the conventional enclosure. It used to be said that the vogue for them climaxed in the late 17th and 18th centuries, but they have undergone a revival of late, both in period or pastiche recreations of historic gardens and in truly Modern designs to which they are uncannily well suited. At the Banque de Luxembourg, for example, the tall stilt hedge creates a sense of lightness at ground level that relates to the modern glass and steel structure of the adjacent *enclos*.

Above:
At the top of this unrealized plan for Castle Howard we see a single area of hedging, solid save for cut-out vistas.

Left:
The stilt hedge at the Banque de Luxembourg, designed by Jacques Wirtz.

Left:
In this north London roof garden that I designed, the focus is the central terrace: a platform of western red cedar decking, which floats above the surrounding gravel bed. This is the void – an area of calm contemplation, kept deliberately empty, except for a table and chairs.

NORTH LONDON ROOF GARDEN

It may seem paradoxical to consider roof gardens as enclosed spaces. High above the ground, not hemmed in or shaded by adjoining gardens, their unique exhilaration comes from their openness. But, more than any other type of garden to be found outside a desert, roof gardens demand a protecting enclosure.

Since they are not ordinary spaces, their design should be extraordinary. When designing this roof garden in north London, I felt that, while the area should be treated simply, there should also be a hierarchy of spaces. The focus is a central platform of western red cedar decking, which floats above the surrounding gravel bed. This is the void – a calm area, empty, except for a table and chairs. A second decked area provides a circulation space as you approach it via the main staircase from the flat below.

My clients are keen gardeners, so the rest of the roof terrace is divided into planting spaces. Growing in a series of galvanized-steel containers are bold drifts of grasses. In their exposed position, they are constantly moving in the breeze and capture the low light at either end of the day. While grasses form the resilient backbone of the garden, within it, seasonal perennials are planted for flower colour and foliage.

The low enclosing wall around the perimeter and other, taller walls are rendered and painted – strong red, yellow ochre, and background grey. The intention was to create something that is quite different from the surrounding buildings. On the roof of this converted factory, my intention was to create an intriguing contrast between a modern open garden and the busy roofscape of the Victorian terraced housing beyond.

Above right:
Bold drifts of grasses have been planted in a series of galvanized-steel containers. As they move in the breeze they capture the light.

Right:
The success of this roof garden lies in the simple treatment of the area and the hierarchy of spaces within the overall composition. This plan shows the balance of decking and gravel surfaces: spaces for dwelling and gardening.

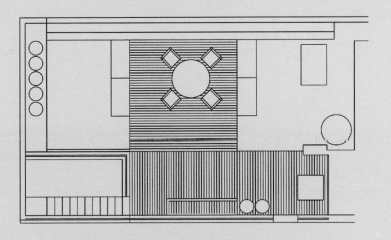

Right:
I created this garden on the roof of a converted factory in north London. It explores the contrast between a modern open design and the busy roofscape of the Victorian terraced housing beyond. Spaces for circulation and seating are decked, those for growing are graveled. Grasses form the resilient backbone of the garden while, within them, seasonal perennials are planted for flower colour and foliage. The low perimeter walls and other, taller walls are rendered and painted strong red, yellow ochre, and grey.

result of a fruitful collaboration between the American architect Richard Meier and landscape architects the Olin Partnership. The building represents a welcome integration of architecture and landscape. Because the Art Center is an environmentally responsible educational space in the Californian landscape, it was essential for it to coexist harmoniously with its context, to reflect and express the special qualities of its habitat. The building emerges at roof level as a series of elegantly produced stone walls, cut mostly from pure white travertine. Within a sequence of spaces, two contrasting areas in particular stand out.

One, a very simple space enclosed by low circular walls and a central lawn with a very pleasing, calm feel to it, is in fact a helipad. On an adjacent roof, which visitors view from above, the planting reflects the local landscape of the surrounding Santa Monica Mountains. The sculptural forms of indigenous American plants, mostly cacti and succulents, echo the unique wildness of the locale and create an extraordinary counterpoint to the urban vista of Los Angeles beyond.

This planting is not only right in aesthetic and topographical terms – it is also practical, for the plants used are drought-tolerant xerophytes adapted to surviving in dry conditions with minimal water. In desert cacti, for example, these adaptions include a reduction of leaf size to spines, to cut down on water loss through transpiration, and swollen stems that can store water. When

Below:
For the J Paul Getty Center in Los Angeles, the Olin Partnership chose to work with, rather than against, the landscape. In a magnificent modern revisiting of the ancient design principle of the borrowed view, they imposed a simple, sculpted, and stone-girt form on a promontory. This helipad overlooks the California hills with all the monumental majesty of an ancient earthwork or ruin.

Right:
When it came to planting the roof of the J Paul Getty Center, the Olin Partnership chose cacti and succulents that reflect the local flora and landscape, need little or no artificial watering, and form a poignant natural replica of the Los Angeles cityscape beyond.

making roof gardens anywhere – not just in the arid southwestern
states of America – water is a serious limiting factor. Due to their
heightened exposure to the wind and sun, and reduced protection
from surrounding trees and buildings, roof gardens experience far
greater evaporation than occurs at ground level. Supplying them
with copious amounts of water, however, raises both technical
and environmental concerns. So the choice, as here at the J Paul
Getty Center, of durable drought-tolerant plants able to survive
solely on natural rainfall, or requiring minimal additional watering,
is a sensible one.

External spaces are also valuable in linking different parts
of a building, particularly in the context of hilly, sloping sites
that offer spectacular panoramic views. It is difficult to imagine
a more spectacular setting than the west side of the site of
the Great Hanshin Earthquake that devastated the Japanese

city of Kobe and its environs in 1995. With a 100m (330ft) drop from the entrance to ocean level, the site, which hugs a 45-degree slope overlooking Osaka Bay, is the setting for a lecture complex designed by the award-winning Japanese architect Tadao Ando.

The architect's idea was to create a series of "rooms" each terminating in a window that would frame the spectacular 180-degree views of the Pacific ocean. This project demonstrates the importance of progression through design. It shows how external spaces can act as a constant reference point, each occupying a position in the hierarchy of the design, from road approach to sea view. It is the external spaces, courtyards, gardens, and pools that bring continuity to the design and make sense of the changing geometry of the entire complex. The spaces themselves each possess their own unique atmosphere and impact, yet the intention is that they should draw you, the viewer, on to the next experience.

It is this connectivity, each space linked as an element within a complex geometry, that liberates Tadao Ando's design. If we pursue that same principle, of creating an unfolding narrative, then our own gardens and landscapes would, likewise, be compositions of breathtaking beauty and freedom.

Opposite and left:
Designed by the Japanese architect Tadao Ando for a corporate building on Awaji Island, Japan, this landscape illustrates Modernism at its most pure and abstract. Surfaces are sheer; lines are almost all rectilinear; planting is minimal. Yet this design is still a garden – and one that succeeds brilliantly in cohabiting with and expressing the maritime topography that surrounds it.

LIGHTING

In this pictorial essay, we see three garden spaces, all Modernist, as they undergo a nocturnal transformation. Within the precise geometry of these gardens, lighting is used, as if in the theatre, to engender cold or warmth, mystery or sensuality, high drama or mellow contemplation. Modern garden-makers should think of lighting as an element that is every bit as vital and defining as solid construction materials or plants.

Right:
At the Portland Art Museum in Oregon, Topher Delaney has created a minimalist sculpture garden of dark and light grey stone. Diffuse but bright lighting gives its sober surfaces a pearly quality by night. An arch-colourist, Delaney has contrived a haunting contrast between the stonework's frosty nocturnal luminescence, the brooding buildings, and the lavender sky.

Following pages:
Created by Vladimir Djurovic for the chalet of fashion designer Elie Saab, this supremely elegant minimalist garden makes optimum – but not maximum – use of three types of lighting. Spotlights paint walls and tree trunks. A pebble hearth creates a night-time focus and summons memories of earlier denizens of this Lebanese landscape. A mirror pool reflects the twilight sky. In a brilliantly planned *coup de théâtre*, all three light sources share the same glowing tonal qualities.

THE WATER GARDEN

Water makes a dramatic intervention in any garden and is probably the element that requires most careful thought when designing. It will always draw the eye and it has an almost magical, magnetic attraction for people, connecting with the subconscious mind and the deepest feelings. It has a mysterious quality, particularly when its actual depth is not revealed and an ambiguity exists between a pool's apparent depth and the reflection of the sky on the surface. Water can also create a wonderful sense of calm and provide an interval between the other spaces in the garden. It is inviting, but it also acts as a barrier between two different areas.

The movement of water draws our attention in different ways. Its animation can be caught by sunlight or by artificial lighting introduced into the scheme. The constant background sound of splashing water moving from one level to another has an effect that is both mesmeric and soothing.

With all these qualities to draw on, the designer is always looking for different ways of using water in a garden and of making it more interactive. Technological developments have opened up many fresh opportunities here, and today's computer-controlled, timed displays mean there is greater potential then ever for dramatic use of this fascinating element.

But it is important to remember that water is also very unforgiving. When using water, a garden-maker must ensure that the design construction is of a very high standard. This is partly a practical matter: pools, for example, must be completely watertight. But there are also aesthetic issues arising from the fact that the natural properties of water have a knack of highlighting flaws in design and materials. For example, because water always maintains its own level, it will tend to draw attention to any discrepancies in its surroundings, such as surfaces and levels that are not perfectly flat.

Symbolic meaning has always been attached to water, and this is another factor for the designer to bear in mind. In the past, its mythological associations led to water's use in gardens as a metaphorical representation of abundance and renewal. This

Left:
Designed by landscape architect Peter Walker, this pond at the Toyota Municipal Museum of Art in Japan surmounts a forested slope and is the central focus of a complex of ancient and modern buildings. Rising from a submerged fountain, air bubbles disturb the surface creating a white circle that is illuminated at night.

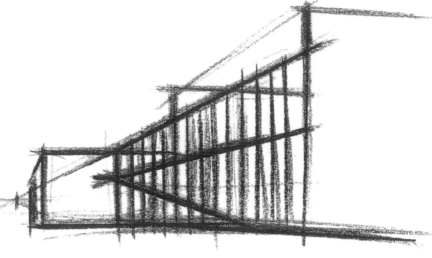

Right and below:
Design and reality: a dynamic drawing (right) made for a house in Chicago by Japanese architect Tadao Ando. Once realized (below), the design offers a wonderful example of water being absolutely integral to a house. A sublime still pool comes right up to the building, connecting its various parts. Left unlit at night, the pool acts as a mirror for the illuminated and fully glazed elevations of the house.

meant that its level was very important. Dried-up ponds and dribbling fountains betokened a form of death, or at least drought. Plenitude and abundance was everything. Even today, a full pool reflecting its surroundings can be one of the simplest and most pleasing elements to include in a garden design, though precise and careful detailing is required if this is to be achieved successfully.

One of the things that sets modern design apart from Classical design is the way in which we use works of art or sculpture in a garden. Art was central to the whole concept of Classical gardens. Indeed, many of them were created expressly to exhibit artworks, hence the siting of busts at the ends of long avenues and vistas, and pavilions set at key points on a pre-determined route. Although such pieces of sculpture were fundamental to Classical gardens, they were, nonetheless, separate from them. Metaphorically and often literally speaking, they were placed upon a plinth.

By contrast, modern garden-makers tend to avoid that separation, aiming instead for designs to which art is integral and where the whole scheme has a unified artistic dimension. In achieving this integration – this single and coherent aesthetic experience – we are greatly aided by modern technology. This is nowhere better illustrated than in the contemporary use of water and all its extraordinary qualities and subtleties.

Designed by the Japanese architect Tadao Ando, this house (left and opposite) brilliantly illustrates the way in which water can be absolutely integral to the composition of the house and garden. A three-storey residence in a quiet area of Chicago, it was designed around an internal courtyard with three wings of the house enclosing the courtyard and one side left open to the surrounding landscape. Two blocks of the house look across to each other and are connected by a long, narrow living room with a terrace on an upper level. Linking together all the various parts of the house is a still pool that comes right up to the footings. In its surface, the architecture of the house lies reflected, complete with dramatic, fully glazed elevations.

This design demonstrates water's ability to contribute to a garden as no other element can. It is a still pool with a base of stones which can be read in, or through, the water. The primary quality that it possesses is reflectivity: the mullions and the ramps that surround the pool are picked up and repeated in the water in a startling graphic composition.

The water also imposes a physical (but not sensory) separation in a way that no other element can. While it connects the house with the surrounding landscape, it also separates it by creating what is essentially a flat terrace, but a terrace that one cannot cross – accessible but inaccessible at the same time. Through ripples and reflections, the water also communicates to us, expressing environmental changes – a sudden breeze, for

Below:
As it laps the footings of this house in Chicago designed by Tadao Ando, this remarkable, pebble-lined pool picks up the shadows of nearby trees and the reflections of the architecture. A brilliant paradox, the pool is a landscape that is both serene and animated, a form of terrace that gives visual but not physical access.

example, or the movement of light around the house during the day, or the shifting seasons. The sense of peace that a pool instills is unequalled by any other feature in a garden. At the same time, this paradoxical element is dynamic: not only does water change in itself, but we derive a sudden and thrilling energy from it, and especially when, as here, we are startled by its presence so close to the house.

Imagine that, instead of using water, Ando had designed a terrace of brick pavers or stone, or a more conventional garden area filled with planting. Either would present itself at once as a huge and intrusive expanse, an imposition on the house, whereas the pool brings simplicity, a heightened quality and a sense of Nature and softness. The result is relaxing and peaceful. The pool reflects the trees that the architect found already on the site and took great care to retain. Indeed, it makes sense of them, gives them a new role and prominence.

At night, a series of different experiences unfolds as, through reflected artificial light, the pool mirrors everything around it. Ando achieved this nocturnal transformation by lighting not the pool itself but the surrounding buildings. In this way, the pool's reflectivity is maximized. This is a master

Below:
At the S'Agaro Garden in Catalonia, Spanish designer Fernando Caruncho has created a water parterre of fourteen pools each 5m (16ft) square. Reflecting the adjacent pine trees and sky, the pools are separated by a grid of stone paths and bounded by low walls. One of this design's most striking features is the single walkway that breaks from the grid to intrude into a pool, so drawing the eye. This detail illustrates the felicity of deviating sometimes from a rigidly regular plan.

GRIDS

Precedents for the modern use of the design grid can be found throughout garden history. Their use was partly a matter of accessibility: in medieval enclosed gardens, for example, the subdivision of areas of planting by paths allowed them to be efficiently managed.

Renaissance gardens were often overlaid by rectilinear geometry which brought an enduring structure to their layout. Much of Classical and Modernist architecture is based on the proportions of rectangles, so promoting a design emphasis that runs in one direction. Although less frequently used, the neutral grid – which is balanced in both directions – can be found in all design periods.

The square was fundamental to Ancient Egyptian and Roman design, and was identified by Andrea Palladio as one of the most beautiful proportions for rooms in his *Four Books on Architecture*. It was the basis of his Villa Rotunda, begun in 1576, as it had been for that building's inspiration, the house that the artist, Mantegna designed for himself in Mantova in 1476.

In gardens, we see the square grid used prominently in the Renaissance compositions of Villa d'Este (1550) and in northern European gardens such as those at Heidelberg Castle (1618). In the New World, the square grid was favoured by no less a landscaper and architect than Thomas Jefferson, the third President of the United States.

Squares and grids of water have been used to create separation in much the same way that moats were used to surround castles for defence. The greatest example of this is Angkor, the city of water and temples

on the Cambodian Lake Tonle Sap, which was shaped at first by irrigation; the whole city was enclosed by a dyke, and became an island during floods.

We see this same principle at work in gardens as at the Villa Lante at Bagnaia, in Italy (1566), and in the setting of the Taj Mahal (1632-54). The Emperor Akbar's Palace at Fatehpur Sikri, in India (above) was built in 1571. Here a massive pool is divided into quarters with a central terrace or island, connected by paths on the main axis. The water presents extraordinary reflections of the enclosing architecture.

Subdividing a surface into a series of compositions was a theme pursued in art by the Cubists. In the work of Braque and

Picasso, images were reinterpreted by being broken up into planes and facets and reassembled. More recently, the British artist David Hockney has worked in a similar way with his "joiners" – works created from a series of square Polaroid photographs – to produce an accurate, yet at the same time, abstracted record. The reflections of a water parterre, animated by jets of moving water, can achieve a similar abstraction.

The Japanese architect Tadao Ando has worked extensively with square grids, for example at the Rokko Housing Development in Kobe. He introduces a sense of ambiguity in his design by overlaying a series of grids, offsetting them, and rotating them at different angles.

Above and left:
In a very large scheme, pools can be used in a magnified version of Caruncho's S'Agaro Garden water parterre. The palace at Fatehpur Sikri in India (above) seems to float upon a giant pool whose surface is transected by elevated paths that run from a central terrace. As a result, the pool appears to be divided and the imposition of a grid enhances the fascination of this single body of water. At the Kobe Rokko Housing Development (left), Tadao Ando has elaborated on this strategy in a series of superimposed design grids.

Right and below:
In his "Flooded House" in
Sydney, the Australian-based
landscape architect Vladimir
Sitta breaks down the
boundaries between dwelling
place, garden space, and
inaccessible water. The main
external area contains a sheet
of shallow water, upon which
the house appears to float, thus
challenging our expectations
of *terra firma*.

Opposite:
An extended trough cuts
through white walls and tree
trunks in a monochrome
composition designed by
the Mexican architect Luis
Barragán. The reflective
properties of the brimming
water create an optical illusion
– a black glassy surface that
appears elevated at one
moment and sunken the next.

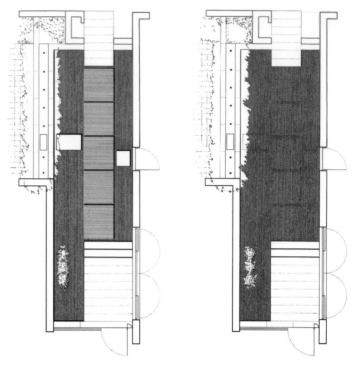

class in garden making; the bold intervention of water right
up to the floor level of the house brings energy to both the
garden and the house.

Equally arresting is Fernando Caruncho's design for a water
parterre of 15 pools separated by a series of stone paths (see
p.96). This is the main feature of a private garden set in the
rugged landscape of Spain's Costa Brava. In this reinterpretation
of the parterre, water is used in place of plants. By maintaining
the water at a high level, the paths appear to float on the surface,
making the idea of walking on them a thrilling prospect.

Caruncho's design is an exercise in simplicity and pure
geometry that succeeds in creating a calm space with enormous
presence. A particularly striking feature is the way in which one
of the walkways escapes from the grid of squares to intrude into
the larger pool – an enticing path that leads the eye to focus on
the mysteries of the water.

One of the lessons we can learn from Japanese gardens is
their pursuit of harmony, both within the garden and with the
landscape beyond. By reducing the number of elements (including
flowering plants) that they use, and by paying extreme care and
attention to detail, the Japanese have managed to make their
gardens both calm and captivating.

Simple materials, such as stone chippings or gravel, are imbued
with unique character by the careful treatment of raking them
into patterns. Serenity is instilled by the precise setting of features,
such as water, stones, lanterns, bowls, and mounds of moss. The
critical factor in traditional Japanese gardens is *ma*, the space
that intervenes between these individual features. In this respect,

they have not changed since a millennium ago when the author of the world's oldest surviving manual of garden design, *Sakuteiki*, defined garden making as "the art of setting stones".

These are gardens that we choose to stay in and to contemplate. But the essence of their mystique need not lie in the nature of the materials used, or in their being Japanese. They are, rather, superb proofs of what, I believe, is a universal truth in garden design: the fewer elements a garden contains, the longer we need to take them in. Because they have a minimalist simplicity we can understand some of Japan's oldest gardens almost as if they were works of modern art. Nor are we mistaken in doing so: these gardens show a thousand year-long process of abstraction and simplification that is comparable to the more recent and sudden development of Western Modernism.

That process continues, fed now by truly modern influences. We see it, for example, in a recent project for a museum built between 1996 and 2000 on a site that is open to the main high street in the Japanese town of Ashino. The commission came from a company dealing in stone and a major part of the brief given to architect Kengo Kuma was to produce a composition that would find a new use for volcanic stone from nearby Mount Nasu. Here the new buildings are constructed from horizontal bands of this local stone, on which a pattern of recesses and

Below:
Designed by Kengo Kuma, the Stone Plaza in Tochigi, in Japan, is a museum space constructed chiefly from bands of local stone on which a pattern of recesses and voids has been imposed to give the walls a three-dimensional, abstract quality. The buildings are arranged around a water-filled courtyard. Its surface reflects not just the sky and its changing moods, but also the surrounding buildings, emphasizing variations in the colour and texture of the stone.

Above:
In traditional Japanese garden design, some paths were deliberately made tortuous so that the visitor would be forced to look down, to take in details that would otherwise be missed, and then encouraged to look up to take in a different view when reaching more secure platforms. In Kengo Kuma's modern Japanese design for the Stone Plaza in Tochigi prefecture, a similar strategy is used – moving from one space to another across diagonal footpaths creates a dramatic experience for visitors.

voids has been imposed to give the walls an abstract three-dimensional quality. The museum is arranged around a linking courtyard filled entirely with water. This creates a dramatic experience for visitors as they move from one space to another across diagonal footpaths. The pools themselves are shallow and their base of andesite – volcanic stone chippings – is clearly visible. The museum can be seen by passers-by, which makes it appealing to visitors, but the large areas of water act as a natural barrier, preventing people from entering the site – so the effect is at once both enticing and controlling. This design is an exercise in calm composition: the surface of the water reflects not just the sky and its changing moods, but also the surrounding buildings, emphasizing subtle variations in the colour and texture of the stone.

In traditional Japanese garden design, some paths – stepping stones, for example – were deliberately made tortuous so that the visitor would be forced to look down, to take in details that would otherwise be missed, and then encouraged to look up to take in a different view when reaching more secure platforms. On this site a similar strategy is used: paths are kept narrow and without protective kerbs or rails. Changes in weather conditions add another variation. After rain, the paths themselves mirror the scene as if they, too, were pools, adding to the endlessly fascinating ambiguity of reflection.

Water can be used to great effect on steeply sloping sites. One approach is to deploy it so as to capture the excitement

of the site, the water cascading over an almost sheer face. Success here relies on great quantities of water, and on the water being animated so that air is introduced. In this way we can achieve the desirable effect of "white water". Without this animation, even large quantities of water tend to be practically invisible from any appreciable distance when they are flowing smoothly over a sheer face.

The water for a fall will need to be recirculated – pumped back up from the lowest to the highest point above the start of the waterfall. If sufficient turbulence can be introduced at source, before it hits the wall, white water will result. Alternatively, the wall can have a roughened surface or be built with a series of small ledges to create the animation; but to be visually powerful, the turbulent flow will probably cause considerable splashing. The sound made by large quantities of falling water can be almost deafening. In a public space, however, this may be thrilling and appropriate: I feel it is important that our public spaces are not anaesthetized from the awe of Nature. Splashing water also has a welcome knack of drowning out traffic noise.

In the Franklin Roosevelt Plaza, Washington, DC, the designer Lawrence Halprin took advantage of the properties of reinforced concrete to make a sculpture of waterfalls and terraces. Designed as a series of cantilevered floating planes, the terraces express the site's various changes of level. Resembling pieces of abstract relief sculpture, they reinforce the experience, and thrill, of water at close quarters for visitors walking around the waterfalls and above the rippling pools.

Another approach is to reinterpret the levels by introducing a regular, calm geometry over the entire site. This method has its roots in De Stijl, a movement founded in 1917 by a group of Dutch artists, and most notably in the work of the painters Piet Mondrian and Theo van Doesburg. Because, in gardens, our approach is three-dimensional rather than two-dimensional, this strategy is more directly reminiscent of the objects and buildings designed by Gerrit Rietveld, also from the Netherlands, and the relief-work constructions of Britain's Victor Pasmore. It has the effect of transforming a sloping site into a Euclidean sculpture, in which the rectangles become pools or terraces on a series of levels. While it articulates the slope very clearly, it also introduces a calm reflective quality, and points of stasis throughout the site.

On the steep slopes of a former olive grove in the Apennine Hills, north of Lucca in Tuscany, the London-based architect Seth Stein has created a remarkable water garden. He organized the space into a series of colourful pools, filled from a high-walled and narrow water trench that emerges from the hilltop and issues from a slot. Water gushes out first into a shallow square pool then into the main swimming pool via another narrow slot. In addition to its visual importance within the overall design, this series of water features and waterfalls provides the soothing sound of falling water – a feature that is particularly welcome in the Apennine

Below:
On the site of an former olive grove in Tuscany, Seth Stein created a remarkable water garden. He organized the space into a series of colourful pools, filled from a high-walled and narrow water trench that emerges from the hilltop and issues through a slot.

LIVING SCULPTURE

I wanted to explore the interaction of stone and water in a garden inspired by our relationship with the planet. Designed as a place for contemplation, this garden is based on the square and the Golden Section to create a sense of beautiful proportion. Filled with water, the site is split lengthwise into two areas: on one side, everything is rectilinear; on the other curved. As an exercise in reflection, the design is an abstract statement about the relationship between water, stone, plants, and humankind.

Two terraces face each other across a long pool. Crafted from western red cedar, they are linked by the arc of a white limestone path. The view from each is focused on a line of giant sandstone boulders hovering over the pool. Face on, the boulders retain the rough-hewn, original ruggedness of the quarry. Their other faces, however, are sheer and sawn precisely to generate a contrast

Above:
My design for this water-filled garden was conceived as a journey, its views and experiences changing with each step.

Opposite:
A line of giant boulders hovers over the pool. Face on, they retain their original ruggedness. Their other faces, however, are sheer-sawn to generate a contrast between rough and smooth, between their natures before and after human intervention.

between rough and smooth, between their natures before and after human intervention. Elsewhere in this garden, sandstone occurs in other forms – as precise sculptures constructed according to the techniques of traditional dry-stone craftsmanship; as blocks wrapped in gabion (wire mesh) cages alongside translucent glass cases; as walls set below the water. The water level is important in terms both of design and symbolism: a full pool, with water brimming right to the edge suggests abundance. In half of the pool I introduced a network of fine jets to create a series of defined ripples. These ripples are abstract representations of water lilies floating on the surface.

This garden is designed as a journey, with views and experiences changing with each step. Only on one's arrival at the far end of the site is the route fully revealed.

summer. Seth Stein's Tuscan terrace reminds us that water is more than a purely aesthetic or horticultural consideration in a garden. We also like to bathe in it and to lounge around it.

The swimming pool has, arguably, engendered some of the worst garden design of all time. In terms of negative visual impact on a garden, few other features can equal the typical rectangular or kidney-shaped pool with its sterile, bath-salts-blue contents and its ugly tiled surround cluttered with soft furnishings, barbecue paraphernalia, and ill-considered ornaments.

As Seth Stein's Tuscan terrace shows, however, this need not be the case. A pool for bathing can be an integral part of the garden rather than an insult to it. In Stein's case, he achieves that partly through the sheer ingenuity of his design, its use of materials and colour. But he also exploits camouflage and ambiguity: his bathing pool is but one of a hierarchy of pools and water chutes all designed within a highly decorative and coherent scheme. In other words, the viewer's attention is drawn not to the fact that here is a swimming pool, isolated and serving one purpose only, but to the existence of a complex of interconnected water features whose immediate message is aesthetic rather than athletic.

At the Casa del Labirinto in Girona, on the Spanish Costa Brava, designers Oscar Tusquets and Bet Figueras have followed Stein's approach when designing their swimming pool. They have reinvented the pool as an artwork on a grand scale, turning it into an elite design feature. In the grounds of the 15th-century villa, they have used bold, dramatic forms to create the setting for a new garden. Again, it is on a challenging, steeply sloping site. The changes of level are achieved by building huge sweeping steps and terraces that draw their inspiration from the expansive, hilly landscape beyond. A smooth-sawn, sandstone colonnade frames a view of evergreen oaks, which, in strong sunlight, is dramatically reflected in a terraced swimming pool that leads away from the house.

Above left and right:
The steps and swimming pool of the Casa del Labirinto in Girona, Spain, designed by Bet Figueras and Oscar Tusquets.

Above:
The swimming pool at the
Banyan Tree Hotel in the
Seychelles is a brilliant
example of an artificial feature
that sits very naturally in
the landscape, or seascape.
The brimming, cantilevered
pool develops the principle
of the unclosed infinity edge.

SWIMMING POOLS AND WATER JETS

The key design lesson of the Casa del Labirinto is that, no matter how conspicuously artificial, a swimming pool must harmonize with the overall design and with the wider landscape. In this case it does so by mirroring exactly the stepped landform: here are yet more terraces, dramatically diagonal just like the others, only they happen to be filled with water rather than earth. Not only is this good design, but it also appeals to something deep within us. Originally we bathed only in natural bodies of water. Why should our constructed swimming pools not summon up that atavistic pleasure?

A sublimely sensuous example of this connection, through design, of artifice with Nature is the swimming pool of the Banyan Tree Hotel in the Seychelles. Why entertain a design that would compete with the Indian Ocean when one can simply steal or simulate it? That is what has happened here in a brilliant extension of an idea that we have already encountered in the work of Luis Barragán. His Mexican water troughs and chutes were designed to challenge our visual norms. Their contents brimmed to the extent that their margins became blurred. Often he chose not to terminate them with an obvious wall. This meant the water courses appeared never to end but simply to recede to a vanishing point, a ruse known in design terms as an "infinity edge".

Below:
Designed by Oscar Tusquets and Bet Figueras, the pool of the Casa del Labirinto in Girona replicates the sweeping diagonal terraces of the larger landscape.

Opposite:
This design by Kathryn Gustafson at Terrasson-la-Villedieu, in France, reminds us that water has precious properties other than tranquillity and reflectivity. Music, movement, and the play of light are all brought to this pool by a series of arching jets.

Below:
Kathryn Gustafson's pool is both an artwork and a garden biotope, intended to support plant and animal life. This design by Andrew Ewing at the Hannah Peschar Sculpture Garden in Surrey, England takes us away from the norms of pond and lake and into the realm of pure sculpture. Here, the principal element of the water garden is water, displayed in an abstract "planting" of dancing jets.

THE COUNTRY GARDEN

The modern country garden is an arena filled with endless possibilities, from rustic charm to radical experimentation. Despite its protean potential, this type of garden does possess some inalienable qualities. First and foremost, it is a meeting place or a transitional zone. This is where the house meets the landscape, or grades into it, and where the successful interaction of the two is critical. The country garden is also where people are most intimately and consistently involved with the green environment: it is a landscape for living. Finally, it is the space in which art and Nature meet head-on. The garden-maker's task is to ensure that they strike a harmonious cohabitation.

A garden I designed in rural Oxfordshire illustrates some of the ways in which one can explore and exploit these qualities.

Within the crook of the L-shaped house, I made a large terrace that sits upon the rim of a gentle slope. While the terrace is rectangular, the rim follows the arc of a gentle circular scoop that we made in the landscape and grassed. Within this circle further concentric forms are mown into the turf so that it resembles and deliberately echoes the ancient sculpted landforms that we looked at in chapter one. On the perimeter of the ring we placed a deer fence; inside this fence, we planted larger ornamental grasses in great sweeping arcs. These plantings capture the spirit of the meadow beyond and create a seamless progression in the design. We go from close-cropped turf within the ring to lush and relaxed grasses at its edge.

So far, then, we have brought together the ideas of ancient and modern (the prehistoric landform and sharp-lined terrace), wild and cultivated (massed ornamental grasses and mown turf), art

Left:
In this rural Oxfordshire garden, I designed a grid of square beds for a massed planting of perennials. The plants were chosen for their naturalistic characters and colours. They were graded so that those nearest the house are comparatively refined in style, whereas those farther away are bolder and capture the spirit of the wild landscape beyond them.

Above:
A circular scoop made in the landscape echoes ancient sculpted landforms. On its perimeter ornamental grasses are planted in great sweeping arcs. These plantings capture the spirit of the meadow beyond and create a seamless progression in the design, from close-cropped turf within the circle to lush and relaxed grasses at its edge.

and amenity (while the garden is a Modernist composition, it equally invites sitting, sunning, walking, playing). This in itself is a modern country garden, but what of gardening?

I made a flat rectangular area, perpendicular to the terrace and, like it, hovering near the rim of the circular landform. This was to be a place for planting, colour, and perfume. Within it we left a single apple tree from the existing vegetation. Its gnarled boughs and picturesque canopy form a link with the trees in the landscape. On the rectangle I then imposed a grid of square planting beds between which ran paths of compacted gravel.

Although this cultivated area is discrete, it was essential that it should relate visually to the house. This we achieved by exploiting the idea of grain or direction in garden design: the principal paths all run away from the house and are clearly visible. A touch of *trompe l'oeil* was also important here. Farthest from the house we planted coarser and larger perennials such as *Eupatorium;* closer to the house we used progressively smaller and more finely textured plants such as *Agastache* and *Penstemon.* This gentle upward grading of vegetation toward the vista replicates the movement of the landscape itself – the eye travels from fine and nurtured foreground detail to bold and bulky backdrop.

As a scheme, few designs could be more Modernist than this one: it is a grid, pure and simple. On the ground and in reality, however, that is not what we experience in this garden. What we feel is relaxation, profusion, exuberance – all qualities that we expect in a country garden. Joyful rather than austere, this mood is established chiefly by the planting in which groups of brightly flowered perennials and tawny ornamental grasses drift among one another. The choice of these plants is critical. The golden haze of grasses such as *Calamagrostis* and *Deschampsia,* the dancing brilliance of perennials like *Gaura,* the earthy tones of *Persicaria* and *Sedum,* all dictate the spirit of the place. As they capture the sunlight, these gauzy and glittering perennials work a transformation, recasting the English landscape as Mediterranean maquis or New England wildflower meadow.

Despite its free spirit, this planting would not succeed without the rigidity of the underlying plan to make it all cohere. In other words, Modernism, so often thought a barren philosophy, can produce the opposite effect. One final point strikes me about the geometry of this scheme: although modern, it triggers memories of things long past. The idea of a distinct area in which valued plants are grown in rows or compartments is reminiscent of cutting gardens, nursery beds, monastic gardens, and potagers. When we

Below:
A grid of square beds divided
by gravel paths creates a
place for plants, colour, and
perfume. An old apple tree,
with its gnarled boughs and
picturesque canopy, forms
a link with the trees in the
landscape beyond.

look at a new scheme, such as this one, we are hearing ancestral voices however faintly. That, I believe, greatly enhances our sense of comfort and connection with this garden.

The Oxfordshire garden interacts with its surrounds through a series of subtle echoes and links (the apple tree in the planted area, for example), and by physically modifying the landscape (the sculpted landform, the heightened ambience of the perennial planting, and so on). In some locations the interaction can be much more direct. In a design created by Topher Delaney in California's Napa Valley, a sleek terrace of pool and paving acts as a promontory overlooking a vista that is the garden's greatest asset. Visually including the surrounding landscape is one of the most widespread and successful strategies in making country gardens. We have already encountered it in the form of "leaping the fence", the trick so beloved of 18th-century English landscapers. That, however, tended to entail creating parkland that was an idealized, edited version of the natural scene beyond. This garden by Topher Delaney is more reminiscent of the Japanese idea of *shakkei*, "borrowed scenery", in which the wild vista forms a key element of the artificial garden composition.

Japanese garden-makers talk of *shakkei* as a form of visual quote from the landscape. Like a quotation in text, it needs marks to frame it, to indicate that while this passage is a part of the

whole, it has a beginning and an end. In the Napa Valley garden, Topher Delaney achieves this framing with blocks of the beautiful blonde grass *Stipa tenuissima*. These grasses physically frame the landscape, especially where a path cuts between them. Their soft, sunlit forms also act as a buffer or mediator between native hillside and terrace. Above all, they represent the distant view in abstract form: although planted within a disciplined and geometric scheme, these grasses exhibit a naturalism that makes them appear to be a literal quote or a welcome visitor from the Californian hills.

These grasses illustrate the landscape frame in its most softly spoken form. It is equally possible to be more explicit, to create what amounts to a physical garden window. Take, for example, the turning circle of a driveway I designed for a large country house in Hampshire that overlooked two types of landscape – parkland close to the house and woodland and fields farther away. The result was too much visual information, too much splendour, for one glance. I felt it was important to separate these two views, partly so that each could be enjoyed in its own right and partly to give shape to the driveway and to screen an adjacent terrace.

Following the arc of the turning circle, I interposed a high curving wall that cut the view in two. Now the distant landscape could be glimpsed, as through a window, via a gap between the wall and the terrace behind it. Meanwhile, the parkland that ran up

to the house was, likewise, given a frame and, with it, new definition. Despite the intervention of a barrier, the eye will always incline to a sweeping view. Perhaps the most intriguing and pleasing result of the wall is that it creates a bi-focal illusion. In attempting to read the view as a whole, we find we are projected in and out, from background to foreground on either side of the wall, in a landscape equivalent of the cinematographer's split-screen effect.

As we saw with Topher Delaney's Californian grasses, it is important when borrowing a landscape to ensure some visual concordance between the frame and the vista: the key to separation is connection. In the case of the Hampshire driveway, I had no plants at my disposal to make that connection – all was hard surface and pure form. Instead, I adopted the tonality and topography of the surrounding country. The brick and gravel I used mimicked the colours of the fields, as did their stepped planes and sweeps the contours of this arable landscape. With the addition of a stone sphere to balance the composition, the result is a wholly abstract, hard-line Modernist design that sits happily within the free and flowing forms of the English countryside. Sometimes the best way to "leap the fence" is to reinforce it.

Mimesis, the imitative representation of Nature or human behaviour, is a fundamental preoccupation of modern art. How can we represent something accurately while subjecting it to a process of fierce abstraction and reduction? Sometimes Modernists achieve mimesis through allusion. Piet Mondrian's famous painting *Broadway Boogie-Woogie* is a grid of largely yellow lines whose colour is suggestive of New York City cabs. My Hampshire walls and terraces echo the pigments and planes of the distant fields. At

Left and opposite:
In this hot and smoky planting (left), I combined bronze fennel (as the major plant) and scarlet *Penstemon* and maroon *Knautia* (as the two secondary plants). In the two adjacent beds each of these secondary plants becomes the major player and two new minor plants are added. This strategy, contiguity, carries across the whole garden (see the green area in plan opposite) so that the grid of paths appears to have been superimposed on a pre-existing landscape of perennials grown in massive informal drifts.

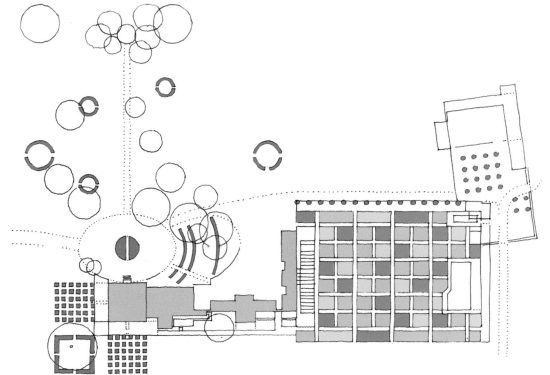

Above:
This driveway turning circle looks out on to two different landscapes – nearby parkland, and woodland and fields farther away. The high curving wall I imposed on the drive cuts the view in two so that the distant landscape is glimpsed through a gap between the wall – this framing device also gives the parkland new definition and importance.

other times, Modernists make art that replicates the essential character of its subject. TS Eliot's poem *The Waste Land*, for example, is an apparently dissonant sequence of cultural fragments and episodes that re-enacts the post-war disintegration of the individual and society. Its form embodies its message: convey chaos through the appearance of chaos.

As we learn from a remarkable landscape created on Rhode Island by Wolfgang Oehme and James van Sweden, this second, literally replicative form of mimesis need not be about disharmony. Here the designers have responded to the challenge of making a country garden by making countryside. This cultivated man-made space is not only inspired by the natural landscape but seeks to imitate it in idealized form. Groves of sinuous multi-stemmed *Amelanchier* emerge from a waist-high tapestry of northeastern US native plants. In winter it is a wonderfully spare and graphic composition; in spring it comes alive with white blossom and a monochrome *mélange* of tender green shoots; in high summer and autumn, the pearls and pastels of bluestem grasses and New England asters gradually turn to russet and luminous gold.

To achieve anything so natural-seeming requires a great deal of deliberation. Oehme and van Sweden will have needed to chose their plant palette with great care, to obtain their plants in vast numbers, to plant them in ratios and relationships that make both

Opposite and below:
In a remarkable landscape created on Rhode Island by Wolfgang Oehme and James van Sweden, the designers have responded to the challenge of making a country garden by making countryside. To achieve something so naturalistic requires great deliberation. Simplicity and repetition, two of the guiding principles of modern design, imbue this space, as does a powerful sense of the poetry of landscape.

SURFACES, PAVING, AND TERRACES

In chapter two (p.35) of *Making the Modern Garden*, we looked at an unlikely source of inspiration for garden design, Piero Della Francesca's painting from the 1460s, *The Flagellation of Christ*. We saw how the artist used a single grid of white-surrounded earthen brown rectangles to structure the ground plane of the painting and to connect its various enclosed and open spaces.

Floor surfaces are among the most critical features in the design of modern gardens. Whether they are paved, flooded, made of gravel, or laid to lawn, they must always possess the qualities of particularity and precision: not only must the material be right for the site, but it must be deployed in the right way. But, as Piero's painting showed us, floor surfaces can also vary within a single site and they can be used to convey vital information, information that will influence our understanding of the garden as a whole.

In this New Zealand design by Rod Barnett (below), we see something very similar to the Renaissance master's ground plane. A grid of white stone surrounds squares of turfing material. This creates a unified surface, a single landscape. At the same time what ought by rights to be static geometry has the effect

of liberating and energizing the landscape: the lines of stone pavers
sweep away in a single direction asking the eye to follow them
to a vanishing point that lies beyond the parapet of the garden.

Vladimir Djurovic (above) elaborates further on the idea of
ground plane direction in this minimalist terrace in the Lebanon.
Here two materials – stone and decking – are used in a mirror
image of one another, sometimes with the stone taking the form
of narrow directional strips running across the decking, sometimes
vice versa. The same materials are then repeated in a different
relationship to form a path that transects these directional lines
and approaches a black pool. Significantly, the pool is designed as
a further terrace, but a terrace with a difference – one that reflects
the sky, cannot be walked upon, and abuts a vertiginous drop.

ecological and aesthetic sense. The result is an artwork that is truly
radical, one that disguises all hints of artifice and instead persuades
the onlooker that he or she has stumbled upon New World Arcadia.
Simplicity and repetition, two of the guiding principles in modern
design, imbue this space, as does a powerful sense of the poetry
of landscape. Paradoxically, this loving recreation of Nature shows
the same maturity of style as a wholly built and plantless scheme
invented by a modern minimalist master.

Here, then, are two degrees of separation – the garden that
borrows the landscape through views, and the garden that borrows
from the landscape by seeking to become it. But I began this
chapter by saying that one of the key aspects, for me, of the
country garden is its ability to integrate with its surroundings, its
status as a transitional zone between dwelling and Nature. At the
beginning of *Making the Modern Garden*, we looked at ancient
earthworks, hill fortifications, and paddyfields as examples of
human markings on topography that have enduring resonance
and beauty. These simple-seeming constructions present one very
direct way in which we can bridge the two realms that converge
in the country garden, human habitation and natural environment.

That is not to say that one should set about making hill forts
or rice terraces; but elemental built forms can have breathtaking
power in rural settings and do much to link habitation with habitat.
The gardens of an old rectory in Sussex, for example, had a broad
area of turf that sloped towards open fields. Here I wanted to
create a space that would connect house with terrain, an open
space for gathering, perhaps. Despite its bare expanse, this area
lacked the essential quality of considered neutrality: emptiness
must be carefully conceived if it is to strike us as anything more
than a blank. So I imposed an amphitheatre upon it, a 16m (53ft)
diameter circle with one shelf or step of seating. This ring may
seem a simple enough device, but remember that the ground
sloped away from the house. Unlike the land, the stone-walled
circle was the same depth and level throughout. This meant that,
nearer the house, its edge was flush with the ground plane, but, as

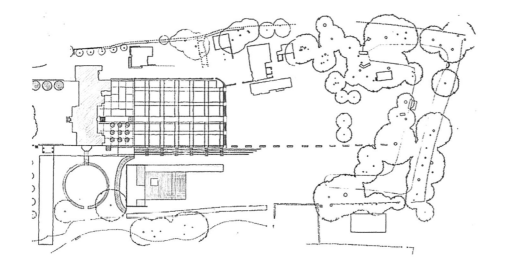

Below and left:
I wanted to create a thought-provoking but neutral space that would connect house with terrain. In a sloping area of turf, I imposed a 16m (53ft) diameter stone amphitheatre. Nearer the house, its edge is set flush with the ground. As one approaches the fields and the ground level falls away, the structure rises above it like a wall. At the house end, a path leads to the amphitheatre and steps down into its interior. At the opposite end, a gap or viewfinder of the same dimensions as the path is left open in the circular wall.

one approached the fields and the ground level fell, the structure gently rose like a wall above the grassy surface. At the house end, a stone path led to the amphitheatre and stepped down into its interior; meanwhile and opposite it at the field end, a gap of the same dimensions as the path was left open in the circular wall. This gap plays negative to the path's positive. It is a form of viewfinder through which the direction of the design flows and finds its outlet, running from house to field and connecting both.

The monumental simplicity of this installation in the landscape is, in fact, belied and greatly enhanced by the carefully calculated way in which it traverses a change in level. This illustrates a paradoxical quality in successful modern design that I think is one of its greatest attractions. The concept may sound uncomplicated yet its realization is technically demanding. The structure can form part of the larger landscape, or (for those seated within) it can conceal the landscape, or it can afford a wholly different view of the landscape as pictured in the frame of the aperture. When it succeeds, simplicity abounds in nuance and complexity.

So a key characteristic of the country garden is that built form projects into the landscape, radiating from the nucleus of the house. The form that radiation takes can produce a dramatic entity in its own right, as we have seen in the example of the amphitheatre. But it can also take less spectacular forms and follow subtler pathways as it navigates the garden, bringing pattern and cohesion to the design. The relationship between these two categories is akin to that between the body's major organs and its blood vessels. Whatever its status, be it a distinct feature or part of the garden's overall system, the materials and construction involved in hard or built form merit careful consideration.

Let us consider, for example, what can be done with a garden path. Presented with the challenge of making a walled garden on a slope, I decided that paths would not only negotiate the design, they would dictate it. I conceived them as a system of broad and shallow steps (see opposite). These fall away in two directions, translating the curvature of the land into a series of long and narrow terraces. The steps are of similar dimensions and proportionate to the rectangular planting beds. These two complementary elements – step and bed – comprise the grid of the garden, a network of planted and neutral spaces.

The planting consists of massed and soft-toned perennials accented by drifts of golden grasses. It is, in other words, a relaxed, generous, and sunny garden. The materials used in the construction of the steps need to have formal rigour and

Below:
Each step appears to be cut
from a single solid material –
I used compacted gravel with
a steel "infinity" edge. Each
riser resembles the face of a
monumental block that has
been cast into deep shadow.

simplicity yet harmonize in tone and ethos with the vegetation. I surrounded the steps and borders with rusted steel edging that possessed some sense of warmth and organic process while remaining sharp to the eye: these are the graphic lines that order the composition. The steps and paths themselves I then filled with bound gravel of a sandy hue to complement the grasses. The gravel was made to fill the steel edging to brimming point. This "infinity" edge has the intriguing effect of making each step appear to be constructed of a single material (compacted gravel) with its rusted steel riser resembling the face of a shallow block that has been cast into deep shadow. This contrast creates an illusion of strong overhead light. It also enhances the stature of the steps, achieving again that desirable quality, monumentality.

It was this same quality that I sought when designing a wall for this garden. Like the paths, it steps down a slope, so I conceived it as a series of descending sandstone steps. Each "step" consisted of a screen of flat-laid and rough-faced dry-stone walling that is united at one end with an inverted "L", a semi-arch made of the same stone but solid, sawn smooth, and straight-edged. These modules were positioned so that the beam of the arch touched the top corner of the next, and lower, section of dry-stone walling. In this way the ancient rubs shoulders with the modern, and the rustic forms a bond with the suave.

What I hope these two examples illustrate is that the principles of Modernism can be readily applied to sites and materials that are sometimes thought antithetical to them. Rural settings and vernacular elements need not imply camp rusticity any more than geometric pattern and purity imply urban sophistication. On the contrary, adapting, say, local stone and craftsmanship to a modern

Above and right:
I conceived this wall as a series of steps. Each of the sandstone modules consists of a screen of rough-faced, dry-stone walling united at one end with a semi-arch of the same stone but solid, sawn smooth, and straight-edged. The modules are positioned so that the beam of the arch sits on the top corner of the next, and lower, section of dry-stone walling – thus ancient and modern stand side by side.

Right:
Another planting strategy is concinnity, the harmonious disposal of similar elements throughout a work. Here, each bed is discrete, an island-like composition with low foreground plants and taller subjects to their rear. All of them, however, contain one or more signature plants. These are repeated at intervals across the whole scheme to create its visual cohesion and atmosphere. Ornamental grasses are ideal for this purpose. Compare this with the strategy of contiguity illustrated on p.118.

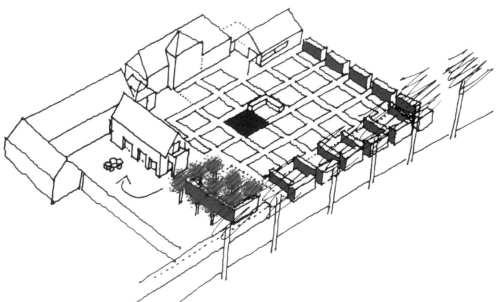

The most obvious way in which a bed within a rectilinear grid can be made to rise above the ground plane is through planting. In this garden, I filled a series of rectangular beds with one variety of ornamental grass. Its dense planting and upright habit create a living, sculptural cube.

design can produce extraordinary results – textures, looks, and atmospheres of unpredicted power and poetry. In this respect, the country garden, far from being the epitome of cosily conservative horticulture, becomes a starting point for radical new departures.

One of these departures takes us into the realm of planting. In each of the country gardens featured in this chapter that I have designed, the plants are organized in a grid of squares or rectangles. It is this ground plane geometry, rather than the shrubbery or statuary of more conventional schemes, which gives the garden its essential structure, its bones. Upon it I then impose a planting that, although varied, aims to generate a single cohesive look or ethos. A grid filled with plants all doing the same thing sounds like a prescription for rigidity and monotony. What ensures that is not the case is the relationship between the different plants as they progress from bed to bed. Creating the right relationship, balancing progression with cohesion and individuality with repetition, requires strategy.

One strategy is contiguity. In the bed illustrated on p.118, we see three plants – one major (bronze fennel) and two minor (scarlet *Penstemon* and maroon *Knautia*) – that I combined to make a hot and smoky composition. In the two adjacent beds within the grid each of these minor plants becomes the major player and two new minor plants are added in turn. This strategy carries across the whole garden so that the grid of paths appears to have been superimposed on a pre-existing landscape of

Below:
In this garden I designed in Hampshire, each bed is offset within a larger but proportionate rectangle. The planting area itself is slightly raised and edged with rusted steel. The floor of the rectangle that surrounds it sits below the level of the paths. This creates a ditch between path and planting. The paths themselves are composed of one type of gravel, while the ditch is partially filled with gravel of another, coarser and contrasting type.

Above:
Variations in ground level and finish are integral components of the design grid. Within their framework, larger variations or deviations become meaningful – as when, say, a pool or pavilion replaces one or several of the planting areas.

RECTANGLES

One of the ideas that I find most intriguing and satisfying when I'm designing planting areas is to create one rectangle contained and offset within another, larger rectangle. It is, essentially, a Modernist idea that was developed by painters such as Piet Mondrian and Ben Nicholson and pioneered by the Hungarian artist and designer László Moholy-Nagy (1895-1945). In this painting by Moholy-Nagy (right), one can readily understand how he came to persuade his colleagues at the Bauhaus to turn from the hectic anxiety of Expressionism to the serene purity of Modernism.

In this painting I find a profound and aesthetic satisfaction in the way, for example, that the single band that transects the lower half of the canvas shifts from deep to pale to medium grey, appearing to hover

over the rectangular form on the left-hand side. That rectangle is itself divided into two proportionate and contrasting areas of tone. The whole ensemble is then repeated in smaller and fainter form toward the top right-hand side as if a distant reflection or repetition of the motif.

In my own planting schemes, I have attempted something like this patterning in three-dimensional form. Planted rectangles are placed, offset, within larger rectangles that are filled, for example, with gravel. Like Moholy-Nagy's foreground strip, a single geometric shape may appear to extend unbroken across a scheme, yet undergo changes of texture, content, and colour during its progress, shifting from planting to paving to water.

In order to translate these graphic Modernist ideas into the third dimension, however, I have had to look back some 1850 years beyond Bauhaus. With buildings set upon pediment-like pavements and their

sunken surfaces bridged by stepping stones, the ruined streets of Pompeii (bottom left) have been a powerful source of inspiration for me. Not only is the ground layer composed of different levels, it also has different finishes, from sheer cut stone to coarse cobbles. Yet each level contains and harmonizes with the next. I often think of these streets when planning a hierarchy of garden surface features such as path, planting area, and pool.

perennials grown in massive informal drifts. The contiguity of the same plant in adjacent beds provides visual continuity. It also allows for subtle chromatic shifts: we progress gradually rather than abruptly from hot colours to cool, from gauzy to grassy, from spiky to *soignée,* and from the bold to the bashful in a scheme of seamless modulation.

An alternative strategy is concinnity, the harmonious disposal of similar elements throughout a work. In the garden illustrated on p.129, I conceived each bed as an island-like plant composition with low foreground elements and taller subjects to their rear. All of the beds, however, contain one or more signature plants. These are repeated at intervals across the whole scheme, ensuring its visual cohesion. When choosing plants that will achieve this rhythmic repetition, it is important to remember that they will bear a considerable burden within the design: they are both principal theme and leitmotif. Perennials that perform over a short season or whose forms and colours are overbearing will result in a scheme that is either of limited interest or overly themed – the much-abused "red" or "white" garden, for example.

Ornamental grasses, by contrast, are ideal for the role. In this garden, I have used *Stipa gigantea, Calamagrostis* x *acutiflora* 'Karl Foerster' and *Miscanthus sinensis* 'Gracillimus' as the signature plants. Each one combines perfectly with the unique plant elements of the individual beds; each speaks to the other from bed to bed across the entire garden; each has a season of interest that extends from early summer through winter. Moreover, grasses such as these, although full of grace,

Above:
For this garden in New South Wales, Australian architect, Glenn Murcutt has used materials that echo the tones and textures of the surrounding bush. There is a leanness, a parched purity about their disposition that is in complete harmony with the climate and ecology of the region.

Opposite and left:
Murcutt's work epitomizes the idea of the country garden as a projection of the house. Although minimalist and modern, this design (opposite) shows a profound empathy with its environment. His outdoor rooms complement the view beyond them (left): the beautifully judged planting, the narrow and, therefore, precious water trough, the varying stepped gradients, the interplay of light and colour – all replicate the landscape in abstract form.

Above:
In this Swedish garden by Ulf Nordfjell the pool is given a dramatic edging of straight stone, a development of a terrace of rectilinear paving and planting. Its surface is traversed by a series of stepping stones that appear to float on the water.

animated, and luminous, possess that rare quality of essential neutrality. As is often the case in Nature, grasses can define and even dominate a landscape without being domineering.

In a Hampshire garden (see pp.130-131), I filled a series of rectangular beds with a single variety of ornamental grass. Each bed is offset within a larger but proportionately shaped rectangle. The planting area itself is raised and edged with rusted steel. The floor of the rectangle that surrounds it, however, sits below the level of the paths. This creates a ditch between planting and path. The paths themselves are composed of one type of gravel, while the ditch is partially filled with gravel of a contrasting type.

Although these details may seem subtle, they constitute small but significant variations in levels and materials that are sufficient to turn a grid into a garden. Within their framework, larger variations amounting to deviations then become meaningful – as, for example, when a pool or pavilion replaces one or several of the rectangular planting areas.

So far in this chapter I have focused chiefly on my own approach to making modern country gardens. There are, however, as many approaches as there are designers and types of terrain.

The work of Australian architect, Glenn Murcutt best exemplifies the idea of the country garden as a projection of the house. His design for a house and garden in New South Wales (pp.134-135) is the antithesis of the "wild" planting on Rhode Island made by Oehme and van Sweden. There the response to countryside was to replicate countryside; here it is to extend the dwelling into the landscape. Yet both responses show empathy with their environments. Murcutt's materials echo the tones and textures of the surrounding bush. There is a parched purity about their disposition that is in harmony with the climate and ecology of this area of Australia. Ultra-modern and minimalist it may be, but this design is more of a country garden than many classics of the genre including Hidcote and Barnsley House in Gloucestershire.

While Oehme and van Sweden and Glenn Murcutt represent two polarities in contemporary country garden making, the Swedish landscape architect Ulf Nordfjell offers us a middle way. His work in rural settings is a synthesis in which lyrical naturalism combines with Modernist features, materials, and aesthetics. For example, this garden (top left and opposite) designed by him in Sweden includes expanses of lawn and informal groups of trees, both favoured elements of the British Landscape school of the 18th and 19th centuries. In addition to these parkland-type features, water, borders, and paths follow sweeping asymmetric outlines

Above:
This garden by Ulf Nordfjell includes parkland features and water, borders, and paths that follow sweeping asymmetric lines. These reinforce the sense of freedom and Nature. Disciplined contemporary principles and materials – including stone, steel, glass, and sculptural elements – are also at work. Plantings of grasses and meadow perennials capture the uninhibited spirit of this place while bespeaking modernity.

Left:
A deck that projects alongside the pool's pebble shore is covered by a slatted shelter of cedar and glass to form a tranquil evocation of the Swedish coastline.

and reinforce the sense of freedom and Nature. Within this liberal regime, however, modern materials and disciplined construction are deployed. The pool is given an edge of straight stone. Its surface is traversed by stepping stones that appear to float on the water. Opposing the terrace is a shore composed of grey pebbles. This is an abstraction from Nature that succeeds both as an echo of wild landscape and as pure design. The same goes for Nordfjell's planting – massed grasses and meadow perennials – which captures the uninhibited spirit of this place while bespeaking modernity.

Talk of a "middle way" reminds me of another, important type of moderation. Although I do not believe that successful modern gardens result from compromise, a design project that amounts to a world in itself may not always be appropriate. Take the example of a fine modern, oak and glass house built on the Berkshire Downs that was inspired by the domestic architecture of the US East Coast (left and below). Here the surrounding landscape had such sublimely Arcadian qualities that it required no intervention on my part. So I confined the garden to the immediate environs of the house. I designed an oak deck that would project from the house and continue at the same level as the flooring material of the rooms. Given the glazed house walls, this created a powerful visual continuity between the exterior and interior. Within the terrace I opened up pebble and gravel-dressed rectangular beds planted with grasses and other durable perennials such as *Sedum.* Like the terrace in which they sat, the plants evoked the dune and driftwood ethos of the New England coastline, the original inspiration for the house. At the same time, they were aesthetically

Opposite and left:
I wanted to create visual continuity between the interior and exterior spaces in this modern, oak and glass house in Berkshire, England (opposite). A terrace of oak deck projects from the glazed house walls and contains pebble and gravel-dressed rectangular beds planted with a mixture of ornamental grasses and other durable perennials. These plants and the terrace evoke the dune and driftwood ethos of the New England coastline, the original inspiration for the house. At the same time, the grasses provide a graceful and harmonious frame for the rolling verdant countryside beyond (left). Here is an example of a comparatively light intervention in which planting forms a link between house and landscape.

at ease within the verdant countryside of Old England. Here is an example of a light intervention in which planting forms a link between house and landscape and reconciles the two.

Few horticultural ideals are so cherished as that of the country garden. But the rustic and rose-bowered popular image is based on a recent invention – in the case of the British Isles, one that did not begin to take shape until the closing years of the 19th century. This strikes me as a liberation. The archetypal country garden that we hold so dear is not an ancient tradition to which we must be wedded. It is merely one way of addressing the challenge of making gardens in rural locations. It is instructive to recall that Christopher Tunnard's Modernist country gardens (chapter two, p.32) were contemporary with Vita Sackville West's Sissinghurst.

The purity of the one and the profusion of the other both have a great deal to commend them. To their qualities, however, we can now add the serene simplicity of Topher Delaney, the naturalism of Wolfgang Oehme and James van Sweden, the abstraction of Glenn Murcutt, the lyrical modern synthesis of Ulf Nordfjell, the fieldstone frameworks of Stephen Stimson Associates, and even my own experiments in marrying habitat with habitation. And this is to name but a few. Of all garden types, the country garden is most often thought to be mired in conservatism. In truth it has become an outdoor design laboratory that inspires boundless experimentation.

Opposite and below: American landscape architects Stephen Stimson Associates are producing some of the most exciting of the new country garden schemes. This design (opposite) illustrates their characteristic interest in combining traditional and vernacular materials. Like many of the modern country gardens we have seen, this is a design that looks backwards as well as forwards and balances the natural landscape with the manmade environment. In this second example (below), again from Stephen Stimson Associates, within the startling concentric arcs of this amphitheatre, irregularly planted trees embody the interaction between humankind and wilderness that underlies all great gardens.

THE LANDSCAPE GARDEN

The phrase "landscape garden" summons visions of artfully placed spinneys, a lake here, a ruin there, and all the other trappings of the English Landscape Movement of the 18th and early 19th centuries. One important modern approach to this genre, however, is more akin to the idea of "negative capability" than to "Capability" Brown. The poet Keats coined the phase "negative capability" in 1817 to describe a state of open-mindedness, "when man is capable of being in uncertainties… without any irritable reaching after fact and reason." The power to evoke this state is one of the great attributes of abstract modern art. It engages the onlooker in its own mystery, elicits a plurality of emotions, and asks as many questions as it answers.

The American designer Janis Hall has achieved this state in several gardens on the East Coast. Her earlier career as a sculptor is evident in the way she reveals the landscape by removing discordant elements and moulding it into simple and evocative forms. In this garden in Connecticut (left), the land is shaped into undulating waves. When we encounter these landforms, we experience a mystical sense of some massive process having been at work. It might be some force such as glaciation, or the fortifications of a long-gone civilization. We can project such ideas onto a vista of rolling crests because Janis Hall has created a work that stimulates the imagination. Uncluttered by associations, we can exult in the landscapes' sheer physicality. Such is the importance of negative capability in the modern garden.

Despite its modernity, this garden can also be seen within the longer Western tradition of landscape design. For example, Janis Hall uses mechanical diggers to achieve effects similar to those sought by William Kent, "Capability" Brown, and Humphry Repton, each of whom would have employed an army of manual labourers. More noteworthy still, her design represents a culmination of the quest in the Western landscape tradition for three elusive qualities. Two of these, "the sinuous line of beauty" and "the serpentine line of grace", were first presented by William Hogarth in his *Analysis of Beauty* (1753). The third quality is that ecstatic and liberating force, the Sublime. As described by Edmund Burke in his *Philosophical Enquiry into the Origins of our Ideas of the Sublime and Beautiful* (1757), this amounted to a new aesthetic

American designer Janis Hall's own beginnings as a modern sculptor are evident in the way she uncovers the essentials of a place – such as earth – and then moulds these into simple and intensely evocative forms.

Top and above:
Janis Hall creates a work
of great simplicity, carefully
removing all intrusive
elements from the existing
landscape and leaving
in their place a terrain of
unimpeachable purity. These
slopes evoke memories,
associations and questions
about the impact of humans
on topography. They are also
a work of abstract modern art.

that overthrew the constraints of artifice in pursuit of heightened feelings. The Sublime drew its primary inspiration from the curving lines of natural phenomena and the vast untamed landscape.

In 1988, the architect, designer, and theorist Charles Jencks and his late wife, the garden historian Maggie Keswick, began work on one of the most remarkable modern landscapes at their home Portrack House in Dumfriesshire. Devoid, in intention at least, of negative capability, *The Garden of Cosmic Speculation* (see pp.146) is the antithesis of Hall's designs. It presents, rather, a clearly identified narrative sequence in which sculpted landforms and built structures illustrate some of the most complex ideas of our times. For example, in the "Universe Cascade" Jencks elaborates on the idea of developmental progression. Here water falls across a series of steps, starting from a sculpted pool. Within the pool, a fountain represents a "white hole" that carries energy back from the black hole of the universe. The flights of steps themselves represent a 13-billion-year time-scale broken into 25 phases rising through the formation of the universe, the evolution of life and the ascent of man.

Yet what sounds like a landscape laden with literal narrative can also be appreciated without any reference to its symbolic content. Jencks explains that his work reflects "the processes of the universe, its energy, its... sudden leaps, its beautiful twists... its catastrophes". His words sound like echoes of Hogarth's "line of beauty" and Burke's Sublime. One cannot deny that Jencks' designs have a single "meaning" that gives rise to them and continues to give them their positive capability. But, in pure terms, they are also dynamic interventions in the landscape that speak to us even, or especially, without all the subtext.

Here are two highly interventionist approaches to the modern landscape garden, but what of the non-interventionist approach? Some of the earliest landscape "gardens" were the sacred groves

HEPWORTH AND ST ANDREWS

I have referred several times to the painter Ben Nicholson when talking about Modernist exemplars for the design of rectilinear grids, terraces, and other surfaces in highly controlled gardens. When thinking about the landscape garden, however, I tend to look not to Nicholson but to his sometime wife, Dame Barbara Hepworth (1903-1975). The greatest British sculptor of the 20th century, Hepworth produced abstract work that was as organic as her husband's was geometric. She looked to natural phenomena such as topography, geological formations, and the outward shapes and intimate anatomy of animals and plants for her primary inspiration. The 1945 sculpture shown here (above right), for example, is titled *Anthos,* the Greek for "flower", and it might indeed be thought reminiscent of the folding perianth of a white arum lily. But this sculpture's true importance lies in the fact that it could be anything or nothing in particular: it might be full of resonances and

associations or it might, quite simply, be a supremely satisfying and pure aesthetic object.

This ambiguity is akin to John Keats' idea of "negative capability", a deliberate and desirable condition of open-mindedness. One of the greatest attributes of abstract Modernism, it allows us intellectual or emotional license when experiencing an artwork without imposing any one "right" interpretation upon us. Some of

the most powerful landscape gardens have this attribute, from the 500-year-old temple garden of Ryoan-ji in Kyoto to the contemporary designs of Janis Hall. They function as intensely evocative and reflective artefacts, provoking our response and projecting it back to us.

This special quality seems to be embodied most notably by flowing natural forms, a fact that was noticed by commentators on aesthetics as early as the 18th century. Landscapes such as the Links at St Andrews in Scotland (left) present a shifting panorama of humps and hollows that picks up and plays with light and shadow. While these landscapes strike us as sculpted, their translation into sculpture did not happen until the advent of abstract Modernism and artists like Hepworth. In landscape design, however, landforms such as this one had already been models for some three centuries, as they continue to be today.

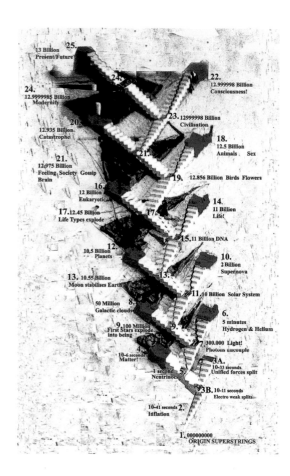

Above:
A model of the Universe Cascade illustrates Charles Jencks' concept of major jumps in evolution over 13 billion years. Each jump is embodied in a platform on a staircase-like waterfall. The water falls diagonally across the steps.

Opposite:
Arising from an excavated pool, the Universe Cascade ascends the side of a hill. A silver metallic fountain represents a "white hole" that brings energy back from the black hole of the universe. Spoil from the excavations has been used to create three harmonic peaks analogous to the multi-universe concept.

of European Antiquity and present-day Asia. These are wild places that humankind has decided to leave alone – except, that is, for activities to do with their veneration and preservation. Our perception of this native landscape is what defines it as a place apart rather than any great changes that we might make to it.

The American designer Steve Martino (see p.150) became disenchanted with the degree of manipulation that he observed in the landscaping of the arid zones of the US Southwest. Intensive irrigation and the introduction of alien plants struck him not only as poor practice but also as a repudiation of the unique flora and topography of these desert areas. So Martino pioneered an approach that would celebrate rather than deny the terrain in which he was working. His designs borrow the surrounding landscape and the vernacular architecture, while his planting consists of desert and semi-desert plants. The resulting sun-soaked, sculptural forms are a spontaneous-seeming intensification of the natural landscape rather than a radical and artificial intervention made in it.

Not that there is anything wrong with artificiality per se. Although the 18th and early 19th century English Landscape Movement style has predisposed us to associate the idea of the landscape garden with naturalism, many created landscapes, from a field pattern to a French parterre, are highly artificial and bear no resemblance to forms found in Nature. Janis Hall's landscapes are an abstraction of Nature; Charles Jencks' are a three-dimensional representation of natural dynamics and phenomena; and Steve Martino's are a distillation of natural habitat. But there is a whole class of other landscape designers who embrace artifice and humankind's wholesale reordering of its environment.

The master of this class is the great French landscape designer André Le Nôtre (1613-1700). Think of his work at the Tuileries and Versailles – elaborate patterns of parterres, allées, and palisades all amounting to a form of decorative, non-representational design that is made with vegetation but without any reference to that vegetation's original state. This is the landscape garden as the triumph of garden (art) over landscape (Nature).

So what happens to Le Nôtre in the Modern or Post-Modern age? We can see his mantle much modernized and worn now by the designer Martha Schwartz. At the Munich headquarters of the finance corporation Swiss Re she has created a series of landscapes that are artificial not only in their layout but also in their elements (see pp.152-155). The theme for much of this design is contrasting zones of inanimate objects and materials – these are used instead of vegetation and to dazzling effect. For example, a

CHALK DOWNLAND GARDEN

In this garden on the chalk downland of Wiltshire, I wanted to create a design that, although modern in its purity and horticultural principles, would nonetheless reverberate with memories and echoes of ancient interventions in the landscape. The county of Wiltshire is particularly rich in ancient monuments, including the long barrow at West Kennet, the earthwork at Silbury Hill, and the standing stones at Avebury and Stonehenge.

Within a horseshoe shape of cropped turf, I set a series of standing stones, an atavistic *coup de théâtre* that might suggest the submerged ruins of a fallen villa or some erstwhile sacred site. Around it I imposed a broad sweeping arc of meadow planting fronted and defined by oak seating. This floriferous meadow band of native chalkland species, including graceful umbellifers, is interspersed with drifts of more carefully coordinated and spectacular non-natives such as the ornamental grass, *Stipa gigantea*, that were chosen for their naturalistic qualities.

As one moves away from the turf arena, the larger landscape is patterned with broken lines composed variously of gravel, hedge and stone. The differing heights and weights of these lines suggest the traces of a former settlement emerging piecemeal from their subterranean slumber. They are the recreated relics or ghosts of those who trod this land long ago.

The overall intention in this particular design is to achieve the appearance of a light and harmonious intervention in the landscape, one that reflects and distills the beauties of the surrounding country, while creating an artifact that is rich in the nuanced poetry of time past.

Above:
Although rough-sided as if straight from the quarry, these blocks of Portland stone are sawn sheer on their upper surfaces, a feature that allows them to act as a canvas for the silhouettes of the surrounding plants.

Right:
The plan of my chalk downland garden shows the rhythmic emergence of broken lines from the landscape. These lines might be gravel, hedging or stone. Their varying heights and qualities suggest the partial exposure of the outlines of some long-buried settlement.

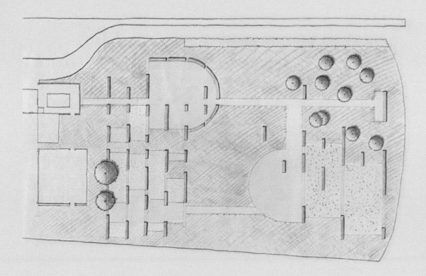

Above:
An area of turf and free-standing stones is embraced by arcs of oak seating and meadow planting.

Left:
Within the meadow planting are drifts of perennials and biennials such as purple *Verbena* and golden *Stipa* that create dramatic highlights among the more muted *mélange* of wildflowers.

shingle field scattered with stone blocks has a provocatively timeless and monumental quality, especially when encountered within the modern headquarters of a company serving a modern industry.

In spaces that lie beneath or within the building and where no plants would grow, she has devised enclosed gardens each of which is patterned by the rhythmic layout of a particular type of object. For example, parallel rows of metallic spheres embedded in a lava-black substrate set off the cool and starkly modern pillars on which the building sits. In a darker interior space, ranks of wooden poles, painted rusty red and laid flat, harmonize with soft and rosy lighting. In another location, again enclosed, lines of gravel-filled rectangular boxes sit upon a bed of gravel of a subtly contrasting tone, forming a unified monochrome composition with the materials of the building itself. Martha Schwartz's plan for the gardens of the Swiss Re building shows that she conceived this series of landscapes as a single entity that runs throughout the ground layer of the site, irrespective of whether one is inside or out. When I look at her plan, I am struck by how it resembles one of the oldest forms of artificial landscape – the field pattern in which blocks of contrasting tone and texture abut one another.

Three or four centuries ago and in the hands of Le Nôtre, these metal balls, painted logs, and gravel boxes would have been clipped hedges and trees. But they would still have been

Opposite and below:
As well as borrowing the view, Steve Martino's designs also borrow the landscape in other ways. His materials echo the tones and textures of the Arizona desert, and sometimes the vernacular architecture of its native peoples. His planting palette consists of desert and semi-desert plants, many of which are indigenous to the regions where he is garden-making. The result is often an assemblage of sun-soaked and starkly sculptural forms that appears to be an intensification of the surrounding terrain rather than a radical and artificial intervention in it.

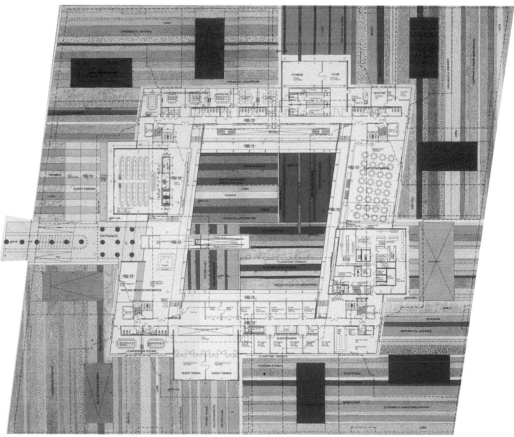

Above:
In spaces that lie beneath or within the Swiss Re building Martha Schwartz has devised enclosed fields – gardens – each of which is patterned by the regular and rhythmic layout of a particular object. Here, rows of metallic spheres set in a lava-black substrate set off the cool and starkly modern pillars on which the building sits.

Left:
Martha Schwartz's plan for the gardens of the Swiss Re building resembles one of the oldest and most inspiring forms of artificial landscape – the field pattern, in which blocks of contrasting tone and texture abut one another.

organized in repeated lines and grids. Martha Schwartz's Swiss Re gardens are a beautiful illustration of the artificial landscape as an art form that has undergone a Modernist revolution while remaining consistent in its aesthetic values and principles.

Artificiality, the wholly constructed landscape, need not imply a complete departure from Nature, however. Another American designer, Faith Okuma, works within the same terrain as Steve Martino – the bright-skied and tan-toned deserts of New Mexico and Arizona. Her response to this environment is to abstract it. In an enclosed garden in Santa Fe (see pp.156-157) smoothly sculpted clay-red walls capture the colours and forms of the surrounding landscape and, indeed, the vernacular architecture of the region. In this last respect, these constructions are an abstraction of an abstraction, a Modernist treatment of local and ancient structures that were themselves derived from the natural landscape and made as a response to it. While it sits in harmony with its locale, Faith Okuma's Santa Fe garden also succeeds quite independently as a work of art, an abstract composition of dramatic and sharply contrasting elements such as the black water chute (an echo of Luis Barragán) and the cut-out terra-cotta wall.

At this point you might ask what makes this design a landscape garden rather than a country garden or merely an enclosed courtyard? While the country garden forms a physical bridge

Right:
In a dark interior space at the Swiss Re building, ranks of wooden poles, painted rusty red and laid flat, harmonize with soft and rosy lighting.

between the human realm and the natural landscape, I think of the landscape garden as a world in itself, as a more autonomous enterprise than the country garden. In this invented reality, we express our ideas and emotions by copying, altering, and interpreting the natural order – and sometimes by ignoring it altogether. For example, I was commissioned to produce a landscape design that would create a special space for outdoor dramatic and musical performances. Several strategies have been favoured by landscapers for this purpose, from the amphitheatre to the simple stage. But I wanted to do something different, to make a building that would reflect both the house and the garden with which it was associated while challenging our preconceptions of both. The result was a structure that we called the *Lyceum* (see pp.160-161).

In the lines and openings of its façade, my *Lyceum* is an abstraction of the back elevation of the house that it faces. It is roofless, open to the sky, and its white exterior walls were conceived to display the projected shadows of the surrounding trees. Apart from producing a shifting pattern of dramatic silhouettes, this gives us a link with the groves of the original Lyceum, that all-important inside/outside place where discussion and recitation took place beneath a canopy of branches.

Its interior is brightly painted and apertures – horizontal slots, an open doorway, and unglazed windows – appear therefore to be blocks and lines of colour recessed within the white canvas of the façade. The values of these "blocks" and "lines" shift with the light: the yellow "doorway", for example, sometimes appears to be a region of solid pigment and, at other times when in half-shadow,

Above:

For this stark interior landscape at the Swiss Re headquarters in Munich, Martha Schwartz used lines of gravel-filled rectangular boxes set on a bed of compacted gravel in a subtly contrasting tone. As these boxes recede, so they become shallower, eventually appearing as little more than frames sunk in the substrate. The landscape forms a unified monochrome composition with the materials of the building itself. Note that there are no plants used.

STRUCTURES

Structures have a long and varied history in the landscape garden almost wherever such gardens have been made. Ruins and temples, pagodas and gazebos, hermitages and picturesque cottages, fountains and colonnades are just some of the more familiar built features in the landscape tradition. Modernism has vastly expanded on this range: long-established structures have been reconfigured in new materials and along new lines, and wholly new features have emerged. Making structures is one area in which the modern landscape garden-maker is most at liberty to experiment and innovate.

For example, a garden I designed for the late Sheikh Zayed (see pp.64–67) took the transforming power of water as its principal theme. Within the garden I wanted to create a pavilion that would act as a connection between an area of irrigation and fertility and a desert-like zone of sand, stone, and xerophytic vegetation. Because water was the theme, I wanted this pavilion to look as if it were made of water, to give the sense of some miraculously crystallized or frozen

cascade or downpour. So I created a structure of interleaved strips of grooved and beaded glass (left). These strips were not sealed, merely superimposed on one another so that air, sound, and perfume could pervade the pavilion. Their layers appeared to shift with the light, generating an interplay of opacity and transparency and echoing the reflective and refractive qualities of water.

Although the construction of this pavilion is complex and technically demanding, its materials are homogeneous and its overall impact is one of purity. As we have seen elsewhere, the resolution of this paradox (complex concept + technical excellence = purity + simplicity) is the key to success in most aspects of the modern garden. It is certainly true of another emerging class of garden structure, the sculptural construction, exemplified here by an enigmatic and powerful object designed by Peter Walker (below). Great thought has gone into the conception and execution of this moon-like mister, yet it makes its impact through its sculptural simplicity and mysterious monumentality.

This page and opposite:
The façade of my *Lyceum* is
an abstraction of the back
elevation of the house that
it faces. It is roofless and its
white exterior walls display the
shadows of the surrounding
trees. Apart from producing
a shifting pattern of dramatic
silhouettes, this gives us a link
with the groves of the original
Lyceum – that all-important
inside/outside place where
discussion and recitation took
place beneath a canopy of
branches. The interior of the
Lyceum is brightly painted and
apertures appear, therefore,
to be blocks and lines of
colour recessed within the
white canvas of the façade.

to be two contiguous rectangles of different tones and depths. But can this building be called a landscape garden? Well, many periods and traditions of landscape design have relied on built structures. Ruins and temples, pagodas and gazebos have all played their part in the story of landscape gardens. You might see my *Lyceum* as standing among them, albeit in sharply modern dress. But I am trying to achieve something deeper than that with this building. It is not just an ornament to the landscape but a way of reflecting, structuring, and focusing the landscape. In the senses of both being condign with it and of metamorphosing into it, the building becomes the garden.

At the Portland Art Museum in Oregon (see above and opposite), Topher Delaney and Andrea Cochran have extended this principle to create one of the most magnificent modern urban landscapes. Featuring no planting other than the surrounding trees, this landscape is entirely built, wholly constructed, a flowing sequence of terraces, steps, and courtyards characterized by sharp geometry, dynamic lines, and materials that bespeak precision and elegant austerity. If there is a sense of "planting", it is in the artful positioning of sculpture, screens, tables, and chairs. If there is a sense of "terrain" it is in the use of contrasting bands of surface texture. These give direction and dynamism to the landscape much as contours do. The Portland Art Museum is the ultimate city landscape – chic, minimalist, and serenely powerful. But I suspect that one of the reasons for its success is that this design strikes a deep chord – the same chord that Janis Hall strikes with her snowy Connecticut slopes.

So we have seen gardens that work with Nature and formal gardens that make no reference to Nature. We have also seen wholly built gardens that exclude vegetation yet still resonate with the spirit of wilderness. Each of these examples stands at a compass point, representing one of many directions that the modern landscape garden can take. I would like to end, however, with a design of my own that takes a more conciliatory approach. It is a new landscape garden at Portland Castle in Dorset.

I conceived the garden as a ringed enclosure, a low wall of Portland stone that echoes the circular outline of the castle. A gravel path within the wall picks up the tan and tawny colouring of the stone and the planting. To my mind, one of the most important but underexploited aspects of the landscape

Below:
If there is a sense of "planting" in the landscape at the Portland Art Museum in Oregon, it is in the artful positioning of tables, chairs, screens, and sculpture. If there is a sense of "terrain" it is in the use of contrasting bands of surface texture that dictate the garden's grain, its visual direction.

Above and below:
I designed this new garden at Portland Castle in Dorset, as a ringed enclosure that echoes the circular outline of the castle. The wall is constructed of Portland stone, a celebrated local material. Immediately within the wall is a circular path of Breedon gravel, a material that picks up the tan and tawny colouring of the stone and the planting. The positioning of the planting, at compass points within the circle is a more cryptic maritime allusion.

garden is the sense of arrival. In this instance, to make the approach to this sunny enclosure a surprise, I imposed a metal access bridge that negotiates a stand of pine trees.

Here, then, is a design that serves to illustrate many of the key features of the modern landscape garden. It connects visually and through its materials and design with the landscape. It draws on Nature directly and through abstraction. It is a place for the free projection of one's own thoughts and emotions: it possesses negative capability. Yet the garden also has narrative content and symbolism, as an expression of generations of earlier interventions made at this site. In this respect, the landscape garden is a palimpsest: our markings overlay those made by other peoples but are never quite free of them. Nor should we wish them to be.

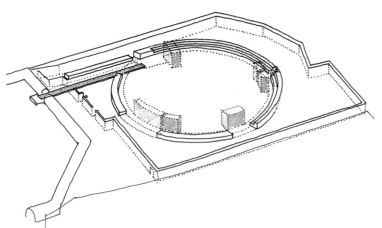

Opposite:
An important aspect of the landscape garden is the sense of arrival. Negotiating a stand of pine trees, a metal bridge makes the approach to this garden at Portland Castle in Dorset a dramatic experience in its own right.

PLANTING:
THE NEW APPROACH

Simply by virtue of their size and shape, trees have more power than any other type of plant to determine the mood and structure of a garden. If we think of the modern garden as an exterior gallery space – in its most basic form, a rectangular courtyard – then trees can serve two functions within it. They can be structural elements of the design. They can also be the objects it contains, the living sculptures. To express these potentialities, we need to apply the same principles that we have already encountered in *Making the Modern Garden*. The trees need to be of a high quality and in harmony with the other materials. If they are to be used in any number, proportion, rhythm, and discipline are paramount: trees should conform to a grid or a repeated pattern. Ideally, they should be of the same type, shape, and age.

If that sounds rigid, then consider one result of this policy. At the Chicago Art Institute in the early 1960s, the American designer Dan Kiley created the South Garden (see p.168), a forum that now links two buildings, one ornate, colonnaded and Beaux Arts, the other Modernist and unadorned. The plain wall of the Modernist building provided a blank canvas for a small informal stand of trees that ascend in a fan of snaking trunks and branches to the roof. Their natural asymmetry complements the austere elegance of the modern structure, generating a pleasing tension. This is an example of the tree as sculpture, a living object that is in concord with the surrounding built forms yet stands alone.

For the forum itself, however, Kiley needed to impose a rhythm to order the space. In the first instance he achieved this by creating a two-level grid of paved terrace and pool, and, on the lower plane, raised beds whose edges would serve as seating. Seen in plan and stripped of vegetation, this design would resemble a Mondrian painting, a composition of squares and spaces, lines and rectangles. The trees that he introduced to this scheme needed, therefore, to reflect its values of harmony and repetition. So upon the built grid, he imposed a living grid, of 28 cockspur hawthorn trees (*Crataegus crus-galli* 'Inermis').

Their flat, tiered crowns provide a canopy for visitors and create a strong horizontal element, a floating band of vegetation that, in visual terms, lies just below the elevated colonnade and

Left:
When framed and thrown into high relief by the elegant austerity of the overall design, few features are more compelling than micro-oases of richly coloured and fine-textured vegetation. In my garden *Hortus Conclusus*, this marshalling of plant life within a few perfectly judged frames illustrates the maxim that is less is more.

Opposite:
At the Dayton Residence in
Minneapolis, the American
landscape architect George
Hargreaves made a series of
elegant "rooms" as a setting
for his clients' collection of
20th-century sculpture. While
nodding to the sculpture
gardens of Baroque Europe,
this double row of honey
locust trees planted in
a graveled terrace makes
a modern statement.

Below:
In the course of a long and
distinguished career, the
American landscape architect
Dan Kiley (1912–2004) did
much to define modern
gardens, and the modern
public garden above all.
Although sharp of line, spare,
and pure, his Modernism
relied on planting. Its
effects can be seen in his
South Garden designed
for the Chicago Art Institute.

reconciles it with the Modernist wall. The expansive nature of
the tree crowns also mirrors the expanses of water and paving:
they are a third and wholly proportionate level in the hierarchy
of design. The trees are all of the same variety, as they must be
to achieve all of the above and to be visually coherent. At the
same time, their repetition is not constricting: while they may
be identical in type, these hawthorns are not identical in every
detail of their branching and outline.

There is an oft-heard anti-Modernist prejudice that in order to
create a garden with a sense of freedom, Nature, and plenitude one
needs masses of plants in an abundance of varieties and free-style
planting. Kiley's Chicago courtyard contains only one plant to speak
of – the hawthorn. That tree is sparingly used within a controlled
rectilinear grid. What we experience is an abstraction of Nature,
an urban grove that is consonant with the cityscape and answers
our deep-seated need for greenery, shelter, and life. Kiley had a
life-long fascination with the idea of the path through the woods.
To walk under these trees is to share that fascination with him.

One group of opponents of Modernist planting is sometimes
unjustly characterized as "plantsmen" or "plantspersons". I say
"unjustly" because, as we shall see, some of the greatest modern
plantspersons are also revolutionary designers and vice versa. For
this often vocal group of opponents, however, modern design is

all about design and destitute of life and diversity. Meanwhile, their own approach to garden-making puts plants first, sometimes with scant regard to the ensuing chaos.

Despite these debates, I cannot see that Kiley's Chicago landscape is anything but a consummate exercise in plantsmanship. Not only are the hawthorns structurally right, but they also provide a succession of spring blossom, fiery autumn foliage, and brick red berries. They are unabashed by Chicago's fierce summer heat, hard winters, and urban pollution. Finally, these hawthorns are native to the USA, Kiley's deliberate echo of the mild Midwest. The South Garden of the Chicago Art Institute may contain only one principal kind of plant, but it is in every sense the perfect plant for that place. It is an apt illustration of the first of two rules for planting modern gardens: less is more. Just as we search for ideal structures and materials, discarding all other possibilities as distractions and detractions from the essential, so we seek the perfect plant.

At the Dayton Residence in Minneapolis (see p.169), the American landscape architect George Hargreaves found his perfect plant in the form of the golden honey locust (*Gleditsia*). His objective here was to create an outdoor gallery, a setting for his client's celebrated collection of 20th-century sculpture. He began by constructing a series of pared-down "rooms" in which rough-textured stone walling and sheer and sharp-edged steps

Below:
Dan Kiley regarded his 1950s garden designs for the Miller residence in Columbus, Indiana, as his best work. In this design, he extended the clean modern geometry of the house into the garden, creating a grid of tree-lined *allées*.

create the outer frame for the artworks. The sculptures themselves
sit upon a gravel-dressed terrace that is reminiscent of the formal
gardens of Baroque Europe. Developing this idea, Hargreaves then
imposed a Modernist reworking of the Baroque concept of the
bosquet, the "little wood", a formal grid of trees through which
visitors may stroll. This needed to be a bosquet with a difference,
however – light-textured, linear, and with sculptural qualities in the
trunks and branching in order to complement the radical simplicity
of the artworks in its midst. So he chose the golden honey locust,
always slim and elegant, radiant in spring and summer when its
dappled shadows paint the gravel surface, and gauntly graphic
in winter when its tracery of bare branches is projected against
the wall. It is, once more, the perfect plant for the place.

*La Nature est un temple où de vivants piliers/Laissent parfois
sortir de confuses paroles.* Nature, wrote Charles Baudelaire in
1857, is a temple of living pillars from which mysterious messages
sometimes issue. The poet's image of a sacred space, a colonnade
of live trunks, is realized in designs such as George Hargreaves'
at the Dayton residence. No other type of plant mirrors human

Above:
The sinuous asymmetry of the
groves at the Miller residence,
designed by Dan Kiley,
generates a pleasing tension
between planned regularity
and cultivated wildness.

architecture quite so literally as trees. To plant them judiciously, as we do when making modern gardens, is to build with Nature, to unleash a welter of profound associations whose complexity is in direct proportion to the simplicity of the design.

This reminds us that trees can be used to define a space as well as to fill it. As we have seen, when it comes to trees, Modernist gardens have much in common with the formal gardens of Renaissance and Baroque Europe and even with far earlier antecedents such as the plantations of ancient Persia and Rome. Modern garden-makers have revived features, such as bosquets, *allées,* avenues, and *quincunxes* (modules of five trees arranged four in a square or diamond with one tree at its centre). They are the walls, corridors, and cloisters of many contemporary designs.

One of the best examples of their use is Dan Kiley's 1950s garden for the Miller residence in Columbus, Indiana (see p.170). The outdoor spaces he created at the residence are imbued with mystery, a living temple whose cumulative effect seems to transcend the genius of even this master. At another level, his method is easy to describe: Kiley extended the clean modern geometry of the

Below:
Modernism has revived and reinvented one of the oldest garden features, the hedge. In this design, the classical box parterre has undergone a metamorphosis. Instead of merely defining a planting space as an edging material, I made the hedge the principal player. It occupies the space in a grid of squares, a monocultural living sculpture.

Left:
Garden designer and historian
Marc Schoellen draws on the
lessons of the past to create
a modern space filled with a
sense of mystery and antiquity.
Alleys of high hedges offer
multiple perspectives and
choices. Artfully placed trees
disrupt their outlines and
generate a feeling that, for
all its orderliness, this design
looks back to some untended
natural state.

Below:
Filling a difficult corner site at
Kalundborg Cathedral Square,
in Denmark, linked squares of
hedging are used in a series
of dramatic diagonals.

house into the garden, creating a grid of tree-lined *allées* buffered by blocks of ground cover, gravel, lawn, and paved terrace. In all of these areas his watchwords were clarity, simplicity, and discipline.

Not every feature of Kiley's Miller residence garden is rectilinear, however. Within the design grid are groves of trees whose trunks have been encouraged to fork and snake. They have also been cleared of lower branches to express their sinuous asymmetry. This generates a pleasing tension between the regularity of the overall plan and the cultivated wildness of some of its elements. To use essentially informal elements, such as these wayward trees at the Miller residence or the hawthorns at the Chicago Art Institute, within a formal and geometric framework is a great coup. It brings us face to face with the central preoccupation of modern garden design: the impact of an abstraction of Nature or the wild landscape on our own artificial environment.

If trees are living building materials that can be used through repetition to create powerful constructions, then so too are hedges. As is the case with Modernism's adopting and adapting the tree-lined avenues and groves of the formal European garden, the craft of hedging has found a place in even the most avant-garde gardens. We have already seen Dan Kiley's deployment of it to create solid, clean-edged walls of vegetation at the Miller garden. This is a clear illustration of the role of hedging within a hierarchy of design. Here, tree, hedge, and low evergreen ground cover constitute an almost seamless green architecture, playing the roles of pillar and roof, walls, steps, and floor materials respectively.

But hedging, or shaped shrubbery, also has potentialities that are entirely its own. It is a medium that cries out for the experimental eye of the modern garden-maker. At one rural site, for example, I decided to invert the conventional concept of the box parterre. Instead of having the hedging outline a series of spaces, I created

Above:
In this garden designed by Jacques Wirtz, the idiosyncratic juxtaposition of two types of hedging expresses the special qualities of both. In winter and spring, the flat-topped, coppery wall of beech contrasts richly with the molten, cloud-pruned forms of evergreen box.

a latticework landscape in which the outline was turf and the squares themselves were filled with low-clipped box. The packaging became the contents. Seen in context, amid rolling downs and distant trees, this parterre is part of a monochrome composition, the various greens metamorphosing from lawn to box to clumps of trees, from manicured cultivation to the relaxed naturalism of the landscape beyond. Once again, less is more, with just one plant used in just one way.

This interplay, or juxtaposition, of the formal with the natural is perhaps the most satisfying of all the potentialities offered by hedging. In the parterre I have just described, pure and geometric regularity is set against an Arcadian vista. By contrast, the garden designer and historian Marc Schoellen uses hedges that are themselves Arcadian and romantically disheveled to create a space that is filled with a sense of obscurity and

antiquity – a brilliantly conceived and brand-new lost domain
(see p.173). His radiating alleys of high hedges offer multiple
perspectives and choices. Saplings, artfully placed though
seemingly random, disrupt the hedges' loose-textured outlines.
Ideas of rationality and orderliness are subverted: is this a new
design or some venerable scheme that has grown unkempt?
Here, a garden of the present seems to look back to some natural
state and forward to a time when it will be tended no longer.

Exploring the formal properties of hedging is a common theme
in modern gardens. Sometimes the formality is pure and celebrated,
as in the remarkable series of linked hedging squares that fills a
triangular corner site at Kalundborg Cathedral Square in Denmark.
Not only does the consciously artificial form of these hedged
compartments suit the built environment, but their dramatic
diagonals amount to an abstract artwork, a living relief whose
ingenuity only becomes apparent when seen from above.

At other times, modern garden-makers have used hedges to
engineer a tension between restraint and abandon. For example,
Jacques Wirtz, the designer who among all the Moderns has done
most to revolutionize hedging, created a double hedge to skirt a
curving sweep of steps (see left). Composed of beech, its outer
wall was flat-topped and sharp-edged. Its inner wall consisted
of molten, amoeba-like box. The beech hedge was classically
European, while the box had been transformed by Wirtz's own
reworking of the Far Eastern practice of cloud pruning in which
evergreens are topiarized into smooth, flowing, and asymmetric
forms. Formal and informal, this idiosyncratic juxtaposition of
two types of hedging expresses the special qualities of both.

In my own use of hedges, the designer from whom I have
drawn inspiration most directly is a man whose name we are
more likely to associate with buildings, furniture, cutlery, and even
cocktail shakers than horticulture – the great Danish architect
Arne Jacobsen. Starting in 1960, Jacobsen designed his
masterpiece, St Catherine's College, Oxford, throughout and
in every detail. This went for the college's gardens, too, which
he conceived as a series of paved courtyards punctuated by
rectangular borders and ranks of free-standing walls and hedges.
Of similar dimensions, the hedges and walls play parallel roles
within an abstract pattern, abutting and alternating with each
other and creating rather than enclosing space. "The fundamental
factor," said Jacobsen, "is proportion. Proportion is precisely
what made the old Greek temples beautiful... and when we look
at some of the most admired buildings of the Renaissance, we
notice they are well-proportioned. That is the essential thing."

I suspect it is the sheer proportionality of this garden at
St Catherine's College that makes it so moving, so monumental,
and so modern. Hedge mirrors garden wall; both mirror border;
all three mirror building. It is a pure and sustained development
of a single theme. Another important aspect of this garden is
that it has direction; like wood, it has a grain, running east/west,

Above:
An attempt to recreate the
plant associations found in
Nature, New Wave planting –
first devised in Germany in the
second half of the last century –
now dominates progressive
approaches to garden-making.
At Westpark in Munich,
Rosemary Weisse, one of the
style's doyennes, has created
a lyrical landscape of grasses
and perennials.

Right and below right: Early New Wave planting aimed to create a matrix of plants in which individuals of different species were planted together in what, it was hoped, would be a harmonious ecosystem. The results, like the borders, were mixed. Piet Oudolf, the Dutch designer (right), and I (below right) adopted an alternative strategy, planting contrasting blocks and drifts of plants rather than mixing individuals. While giving the plants sufficient space and critical mass to thrive and to withstand competition, this approach also makes greater aesthetic sense: the eye reads sweeps and blocks of colour far more easily than it does a mass of discordant detail.

right/left in a majestic horizontal the length of the buildings. The rows of hedges are essential in establishing that grain: they all point the same way. This is an idea that I have found invaluable.

So far we have considered trees and hedges as stand-alone elements of modern gardens. They can, however, be combined with each other and with other types of plants such as flowering shrubs and herbaceous perennials. One of my own aims in making modern gardens is to integrate these three classes of vegetation – tree, hedge, and soft planting – within a hierarchy of design where each plays an essential role. In doing so, I see the plants as building blocks within a scheme rather than mere adornments to it.

This is best illustrated by *Hortus Conclusus,* a garden I created at the 2004 Chelsea Flower Show (see pp.166–167). Designed on a grid, the garden occupied a small, tightly controlled space. Amid rectilinear areas of paving, planting, pools, and narrow rills, six plane trees (*Platanus*) stood two abreast to create a central canopy. Their stems were cleared in stilt hedge style to reveal the beauty of the bark, while their crowns were pruned into squares to produce a sheltering rectangle of elevated foliage. Clipped hornbeam hedging (*Carpinus betulus*) formed a series of living walls. Rectangular and all of the same height and width, these reflected the geometry of the hard features. The hedges were placed on the grid in a seemingly random sequence, sometimes overlapping, sometimes running on one from another, to create glimpsed views and multiple perspectives. Their randomness was illusory: in fact, all of these hedges ran in the same direction, from front to back along the axis of the design. In this way, they articulated the grain of the garden by lifting the ground plane into the third dimension.

These two species, plane and hornbeam, tree and hedge, endow the garden with its structure. They are living building materials. They are also, of course, capable of being pruned

and trained to rectilinear shapes. The same cannot be said for the third category of vegetation that I introduced to this garden, a floriferous and consciously informal mix of vintage roses, grasses, and perennials. How does one deploy plants such as these without detracting from the purity and discipline of the design?

In a sequence of beds, I planted a matrix of ornamental grasses. These furnished an airy foil for a pointillist composition, an apparently random selection of old roses and perennials. The repetition of the grasses as a constant also provided an internal context. So too did the repetition at intervals of the same colour even when presented by different plants – for example, the velvety ruby of both *Knautia macedonica* and *Rosa* 'Tuscany Superb'. Moreover, the hues of the roses and perennials, although varied, were harmonious: shades of ruby, pink, crimson, maroon, mauve, sapphire, and azure sat side by side in a jewel box of plants.

Perhaps the most critical factor in this approach to planting, however, is that word "box". The borders in this Chelsea garden were rectangular, echoing the lines of the hard features and clipped trees and hedging. Although deliberately unruly within their own confines, the beds functioned as orderly elements within the hierarchy of design. Not only do boxes such as these convert chaos into cosmos, they also enhance the power of the plants themselves. Rich colour, free-flowing forms, abundance, wildness, and romance are more moving when contained and

Below:
At Hummelo, his garden and nursery in the Netherlands, Piet Oudolf experiments with the main ingredients of the new approach to planting, hardy herbaceous perennials. Some of these, such as *Veronicastrum* and *Echinops* (foreground, left and right respectively), are familiar to gardeners, but are reselected and refined by Oudolf and cast in new roles. Others, such as various *Sanguisorba* species (midground right), have only recently been introduced to cultivation.

concentrated. In elegant but austere modern gardens where hard surfaces predominate and vegetation is pared down, few features are more compelling than these micro-oases. This marshalling of plant life within a few frames is another illustration of the rule that less is more. It also brings us to the second rule of the new approach to planting which, paradoxically, is that more is more.

When describing the ornamental grasses in my Chelsea garden *Hortus Conclusus,* I used the term "matrix". In its earliest sense, a matrix was a womb. It has, however, acquired other senses since the Middle Ages and in many fields, from mineralogy to mathematics. If we think of a matrix as an area of undifferentiated mother tissue from which phenomena arise – like crystals in a bed of coarse sedimentary rock – then we begin to approach its horticultural meaning. That meaning was first defined in Germany towards the end of the last century when, looking for a new approach to planting, horticulturists took a lesson from ecology. Ecologists assess a habitat by counting and studying the different species found within a quadrat, a square sample area that is representative of the whole. In a meadow or prairie quadrat, grasses tend to predominate while other flowering perennials appear more sporadically. The new German school of planting attempted to simulate habitats in the garden by using plants such as grasses and other hardy herbaceous perennials in ratios and relationships of the kind that one might discern in Nature. They created a module, a garden quadrat, that could be repeated to form an overall design. They termed this a "matrix" because it

Above:
If any one group of perennials is identified with the new approach to planting, it is ornamental grasses. Here, I've combined two *Stipa* species, *Stipa gigantea* (top right corner) and *Stipa tenuissima* (massed throughout). Their presence is both neutral, as a foil for more colourful perennials, and uniquely characterful: no other plants impart light, grace, and movement to a scheme in the same way.

Above:
The new approach to planting pays homage to Nature by replicating its habitats and processes and attempting to garden without insult to the environment. For all that, it remains a consciously artistic, not to say painterly, design philosophy. It has, for example, ushered in an exciting new era of colour experiments – as in this garden made by British designer Dan Pearson, which is a treasure house of topaz *Eremurus,* gilded *Stipa,* and garnet *Knautia macedonica.*

tended to consist chiefly of grasses among which more colourful perennials would be dotted. Matrix planting was a beautiful idea that re-established the link between the wild and cultivated realms.

This new theory succeeded in making us reassess the value of certain plants and the role of naturalism in the garden. Chief among the rediscovered plants were ornamental grasses, soon followed in the order of precedence by prairie and other grassland perennials, members of the daisy family, such as *Aster, Echinacea,* and *Rudbeckia,* Lamiaceae like *Monarda* and *Origanum,* and Scrophulariaceae such as *Verbascum.* The lasting lesson of the matrix was that grasses were an ideal foundation for planting. Set amid their softly sparkling colours and graceful lines, other more flamboyant perennials suddenly acquired beauty and purpose.

Just as garden design was becoming unashamedly Modernist in embracing purity and austerity, modern planting was turning to Nature and profusion. Although that sounds like a parting of the ways, the two trends are in fact strongly sympathetic. As we saw in my Chelsea garden, *Hortus Conclusus,* a mixed matrix-style planting of grasses and flowering perennials can float within a cool and highly structured design like a vivid quote from Nature. In larger schemes, this combination of graceful blade and brilliant bloom can completely structure a landscape: grasses may bespeak wildness, freedom, and movement yet they are nothing if not architectural. They are building blocks – in design terms, the herbaceous equivalent of trees and hedges – and, like the best modern materials, they possess an essential neutrality.

Early attempts to create matrices that copied natural ecosystems were not always sustainable. It was the Dutch plantsman and designer Piet Oudolf who pioneered a successful solution. He began planting grasses and perennials in contrasting blocks and drifts, each of which consisted of one variety only. This achieved the appearance of nature while giving the plants sufficient space and volume to thrive. If we look at Oudolf's Millennium Garden at Pensthorpe Waterfowl Park, in Norfolk, for example, we see a landscape that is alive with the spirit of Nature. It is also a low-maintenance sustainable scheme.

Toward the end of the last century, this approach was termed the New Wave Perennials movement. In schemes where we want plants to predominate, it continues to be the dominant style in

Below:
At Bury Court in Hampshire, England, plantsman John Coke created this elegant planting of ornamental grasses, pin-point perennials such as *Dianthus carthusianorum,* and topiary. It is a brilliant marriage of the freedom of the new approach to planting and the pure restraint of Modernism.

modern garden planting. The key to the New Wave is more is more – achieving that critical mass of any given plant which will secure good design and good horticulture. There is, for example, little point even in a small garden in planting one *Miscanthus* beside one *Echinacea* beside one *Sedum.* Plant five of each, however, and you begin to make a picture that is informed with the principles of modern design: rhythm and repetition, purity of form, abstraction from Nature.

In my own work, I often apply these principles even more strictly to planting than is usual in the New Wave style. In a garden surrounding a pavilion at Bury Court, in Hampshire, for example, the owner, plantsman John Coke, and I confined ourselves largely to grasses (see p.132). Although this is a strongly structured scheme involving a grid of square beds and pools that complements the geometry of the pavilion, it is filled with freedom, light, and movement. The flowing forms of the grasses suggest a reedbed. They are planted in volume in what is essentially a monochrome composition, yet their similarities are soon supplanted by a growing awareness of their different qualities. In other words, the scheme delivers both a single and immediate visual impact and a gradual engagement with subtlety, diversity, and detail.

But what if you garden in an area where grasses and other darlings of the New Wave movement are ruled out by climatic conditions, or, perhaps, you simply do not like them? At Elmstead

Below:
Few natural habitats have had greater influence on the new approach to planting than the North American prairie. In recent years, European gardens have begun to fill with late summer-flowering daisies, grasses, and other perennials that have been either newly introduced from the USA or revived after decades of undeserved neglect. Neil Diboll, President of the Prairie Nursery in Wisconsin, is one of their great champions. Liberated, lyrical, and luminous, this Texas wildflower meadow planted by him shows exactly the qualities that make these plants, and this look, so desirable.

Above:
Sun-loving plants in informal beds spill seamlessly into the gravel surrounds at Beth Chatto's gravel garden at Elmstead Market, in Essex.

Left:
For the layout of this parterre, designer Tom Stuart-Smith used a microscopic image of the structure of a tree leaf found on site. So an old motif (the parterre) is transformed through a new technique (microscopy), and an artificial introduction to the landscape is modeled on one of its wild and original elements.

Market in Essex, the great plantswoman Beth Chatto copes with some of the lowest rainfall in the United Kingdom. In 1992, she decided to make an opportunity of adversity by creating a gravel garden. A symphonic sequence of informal beds where sun-lovers spill seamlessly into the shingle surrounds, it bears all the characteristics of the best modern planting. Plants are chosen for their compatibility with each other and with their given environment. They are planted chiefly in drifts that build beautifully modulated chromatic harmonies. The garden appears naturalistic, free in form, and open to some degree of autonomous change. In the choice and balance of its materials, however, and in the purity of its conception, it is the product of great planning and painstaking design.

A garden such as Pensthorpe or Elmstead Market proves that plantsmanship and ground-breaking design can go hand in hand. Moving from the east of England to California and an even more challenging climate, we find the same marriage, where the small-scale, slate and succulent schemes of Isabelle Greene resemble a landscape viewed from the air, and where the Desert Garden at the Huntington Library in San Marino assumes the appearance of a living sculpture park.

These gardens demonstrate that the new approach to planting can be applied no matter where the site is. In each case it is the tones and textures of plants that give the garden its unique character and structure. But then Nature is the best designer – even when it contains no plants, if a modern garden is to succeed, her influence must not be far away.

Above and left:
In a process of abstraction that is reminiscent of some traditional Japanese gardens, American designer Isabelle Greene looks to the natural landscape for inspiration. In this Californian garden, the textures and colours of the arid American southwest are translated into patterns of slate, shingle and succulents.

Opposite page:
Started in 1925, the Desert Garden at the Huntington Library and Botanical Gardens, California, is the largest collection of cacti and succulents in the world. It succeeds brilliantly as a modern design. First, the plants are ideal for the site and require minimal watering and maintenance. Second, they are displayed in such a way that it is chiefly their forms that give this garden its unique character and structure.

BIBLIOGRAPHY

GARDENS AND LANDSCAPES IN GENERAL

Griffiths, M; Huxley, A; Levy, M (editors), 1992, *The New Royal Horticultural Society Dictionary of Gardening*

Hobhouse, P, 2002, *The Story of Gardening*

Jellicoe, G; Jellicoe, S, 1987, *The Landscape of Man*

Mosser, M; Teyssot, G, 1990, *The History of Garden Design: The Western Tradition from the Renaissance to the Present Day*

Taylor, P (ed), 2006, *The Oxford Companion to the Garden*

MODERN GARDENS AND LANDSCAPES

Amidon, J; Gustafson, K, 2003, *Radical Landscapes: Reinventing Outdoor Space*

Boettger, S, 2004, *Earthworks: Art and the Landscape of the Sixties*

Brown, J, 1999, *The English Garden through the 20th Century*

Brown, J, 2000, *The Modern Garden*

Cane, P, 1926, *Modern Gardens, British and Foreign*

Condon, P; Neckar, L (editors), 1990, *The Avant-Garde and the Landscape: Can They Be Reconciled?*

Cooper, G; Taylor, G, 1996, *Paradise Transformed: the Private Garden for the Twenty-first Century*

Cooper, G; Taylor, G, 2000, *Gardens for the Future*

Deunk, G, 2001, *20th Century Garden and Landscape Architecture in the Netherlands*

Imbert, D, 1993, *The Modernist Garden in France*

Jellicoe, G, 1960, *Studies in Landscape Design*

Jellicoe, G; Jellicoe, S, 1968, *Modern Private Gardens*

Kassler, E, 1964 (revised 1984), *Modern Gardens and the Landscape*

Kastner, J; Wallis, B (editors), 2005, *Land and Environmental Art (Themes & Movements)*

Martin, R (editor), 1990, *The New Urban Landscape*

McHarg, I, 1969 (reissued 1971) *Design with Nature*

Plumptre, G, 1988, *The Latest Country Gardens*

Reed, P, 2005, *Groundswell: Constructing the Contemporary Landscape*

Relph, E, 1987, *The Modern Urban Landscape: 1880 to the Present*

Richardson, T, 2005, *English Gardens in the Twentieth Century*

Rico Nose, M, 2002, *The Modern Japanese Garden*

Saward, J, 2002, *Magical Paths: Labyrinths & Mazes in the 21st Century*

Shepheard, P, 1953, *Modern Gardens*

Snape, D (editor), 2003, *The Australian Garden: Designing with Australian Plants*

Streatfield, D, 1994, *California Gardens*

Taylor, G, 1946 (3rd edition), *The Modern Garden*

Treib, M (editor), 1994, *Modern Landscape Architecture: A Critical Review*

Turner, T, 1995, *City as Landscape: A Post-modern View of Design and Planning*

Waymark, J, 2005, *Modern Garden Design: Innovation Since 1900*

Whiston Spirn, A, 2000 (paperback edition), *The Language of Landscape*

Wilson A, 2002, *Influential Gardeners: the Designers who shaped 20th Century Garden Style*

WORKS ON OR BY MODERN DESIGNERS

Altshuler, B, 1994, *Isamu Noguchi*

Amidon, J; Gustafson, K, 2005, *Moving Horizons: the Landscape Architecture of Kathryn Gustafson & Partners*

Amidon, J, 2006, *Peter Walker and Partners (Source Books in Landscape Architecture, no. 3)*

Ando, T; Heneghan, T; Pare, R, 2000, *Tadao Ando: The Colours of Light*

Ashton, D, 1993, *Noguchi: East and West*

Bradley-Hole, C, 1999, *The Minimalist Garden*

Brookes, J, 1969, *Room Outside*

Brookes, J, 2001 (2nd edition), *Garden Design*

Brown, J, 1982, *Gardens of a Golden Afternoon – the Story of a Partnership: Edwin Lutyens & Gertrude Jekyll*

Brown, J, 1985, *Vita's Other World: a Garden Biography of Vita Sackville-West*

Brown, J, 1987, *Lanning Roper and his Gardens*

Burri, R, 2004, *Luis Barragán*

Chatto, B, 2000, *Beth Chatto's Gravel Garden*

Church, T, 1955, *Gardens are for People*

Clément, G, 1997, *Les Libres Jardins de Gilles Clément*

Collens, G; Powell, W (editors), 1999, *Sylvia Crowe*

Colvin, B, 1947, *Land and Landscape*

Cooper, G; Taylor, G, 2000, *Mirrors of Paradise: the Gardens of Fernando Caruncho*

Cotter, S (editor), 2002, *How to Be Modern: Arne Jacobsen in the 21st Century*

Crowe, S, 1956, *Tomorrow's Landscape*

Crowe, S, 1958 (revised 1994), *Garden Design*

Delaney, T; Grayson Trulove, J (editors), 2001, *Ten Landscapes: Topher Delaney*

Eckbo, G, 1956, *The Art of Home Landscaping*

Eckbo, G, 1969, *The Landscape We See*

Eliovson, S, 1991, *The Gardens of Roberto Burle Marx*

Frampton, K, 2003, *Tadao Ando: Light and Water*

Halprin, L, 1963 (reissued 1972), *Cities*

Hooker, D; Moorhouse, P, 2005, *Richard Long: Walking the Line*

Jacobsen, A, 2003, *Arne Jacobsen – Absolutely Modern*

Jarman, D, 1995, *Derek Jarman's Garden*

Jellicoe, G; Sutherland, L, 1991, *Designing the New Landscape*

Jencks, C, 2003, *The Garden of Cosmic Speculation*

Jodidio, P, 2004, *Tadao Ando*

Karson, R, 1989, *Fletcher Steele, Landscape Architect*

Kienast, D, 1997, *Gardens*

Kienast, D; et al, 2000, *Open Spaces*

Kienast, D, 2001, *Parks and Cemeteries*

Kiley, D; Amidon, J, 2003, *Dan Kiley: the Complete Works of America's Master Landscape Architect*

Levy, L, 1997, *Kathryn Gustafson: The Modern French Garden*

Noguchi, I, 1987, *Garden Museum*

Oehme, W; Van Sweden, J, 1998, *Bold Romantic Gardens*

Page, R, 1962, *The Education of a Gardener*

Richardson, T (editor), 2004, *The Vanguard Landscapes and Designs of Martha Schwartz*

Sheeler, J, 2003, *Little Sparta: the Garden of Ian Hamilton Finlay*

Simo, M; Walker, P, 1994, *Invisible Gardens*

Siza, A, 2003, *Barragán: the Complete Works*

Spens, M, 1992, *Gardens of the Mind: the Genius of Geoffrey Jellicoe*

Spens, M, 1993, *Jellicoe at Shute*

Spens, M, 1994, *The Complete Landscape Designs and Gardens of Geoffrey Jellicoe*

Steele, F, 1930, *New Pioneering in Landscape Design*

Steele, F, 1932, *Landscape Design of the Future*

Steele, F, 1936, *Modern Landscape Design*

Taylor, P, 2003, *The Wirtz Gardens*

Treib, M; Imbert, D, 1997, *Garrett Eckbo: Modern Landscapes for Living*

Treib, M, 2004, *Thomas Church, Landscape Architect: Making a Modern Californian Landscape*

Tunnard, C, 1938, *Gardens in the Modern Landscape*

Weilacher, U, 2001, *Visionary Gardens: Modern Landscapes by Ernst Cramer*

INFLUENCES FROM OTHER CULTURES AND ERAS

Brookes, J, 1987, *Gardens of Paradise: History and Design of the Great Islamic Gardens*

Daniels, S, 1999, *Humphry Repton: Landscape Gardening and the Geography of Georgian England*

Dixon Hunt, J, 1987, *William Kent: Landscape Garden Designer*

Hamilton Hazlehurst, F, 1980, *Gardens of Illusion: the Genius of André Le Nostre (Le Nôtre)*

Hobhouse, P, 2003, *Gardens of Persia*

Keane, M, 1996, *Japanese Garden Design*

Keswick, M, 2002 (revised edition), *The Chinese Garden – History, Art, and Architecture*

Ito, T, 1972, *The Japanese Garden: an Approach to Nature*

Lazzaro, C, 1990, *The Italian Renaissance Garden*

Moynihan, E, 1980, *Paradise as a Garden in Persia and Mughal India*

Stroud, D, 1975, *Capability Brown*

PLANTS AND PLANTING

Brickell, C, 2003 (3rd edition), *The RHS A–Z Encyclopedia of Garden Plants* (2 volumes)

Christopher, M, 2006, *Late Summer Flowers*

Clausen, R; Ekstrom, N, 1989, *Perennials for American Gardens*

Darke, R, 1999, *The Colour Encyclopedia of Ornamental Grasses*

Darke, R; Griffiths, M (editors), 1994, *The RHS Manual of Grasses*

Gerritsen, H; Oudolf, P, 2001, *Dream Plants for the Natural Garden*

Griffiths M, 1994, *The Royal Horticultural Society Index of Garden Plants*

Hillier Nurseries, 2002 (8th edition), *The Hillier Manual of Trees and Shrubs*

Joyce, D, 1999, *Topiary and the Art of Training Plants*

King, M; Oudolf, P, 1996, *Gardening with Grasses*

Kingsbury, N, 1996, *The New Perennial Garden*

Kingsbury, N; Oudolf, P, 1999, *Designing with Plants*

Kingsbury, N; Oudolf, P, 2005, *Planting Design: Gardens in Time and Space*

Lewis, P, 2003, *Making a Wildflower Meadow*

Oudolf, P, 2003, *Planting the Natural Garden*

Quest-Ritson, B; Quest-Ritson, C, 2003, *The RHS Encyclopedia of Roses*

Rice, G (editor), 2006, *The Royal Horticultural Society Encyclopedia of Perennials*

Wiley, K, 2004, *On the Wild Side: Experiments in New Naturalism*

INDEX

ACKNOWLEDGMENTS

Mitchell Beazley would like to thank the following people for supplying photographs.

Page 1 Harpur Garden Library/Jerry Harpur/ Design: Christopher Bradley-Hole; **2/3** Christopher Bradley-Hole; **5** Vladimir Djurovic Landscape Architecture; **7** Andrew Lawson Photography/ Design: Christopher Bradley-Hole; **8–9** Courtesy of Richard Long and Haunch of Venison; **10** Corbis/ © Angelo Hornak; **11** Harpur Garden Library/Jerry Harpur; **12** Corbis/© Bennett Dean, Eye Ubiquitous; **13 top** Network Photographers Ltd/Georg Gerster; **13 bottom** Alamy/Iain Masterton; **14–15** Corbis/ Ed Kashi; **16** Bridgeman Art Library/Collection of the Earl of Leicester, Holkham Hall, Norfolk; **17** Bridgeman Art Library/Museo di Firenze Com'era, Florence; **18** Art Archive/Dagli Orti; **19** Corbis/© Francesco Venturi; Kea Publishing Services Ltd/© DACS 2004; **20** Bridgeman Art Library/Private Collection/© FLC/ADAGP, Paris, and DACS, London 2004; **21 top** Garden Exposures Photo Library/© Andrea Jones Location Photography; **21 bottom** Arch Haruyoshi Ono – Burle Marx & Cia Ltda; **22** © Tate, London/ © Angela Verren-Taunt 2004. All Rights Reserved, DACS; **23** © Tate, London/© Carl Andre/VAGA, New York/DACS, London 2004; **24** Serpentine Gallery/Photo: Stephen White/© ARS, NY, and DACS, London 2004; **25** Kunsthaus Zürich/ © Richard Paul Lohse Foundation, Zürich/DACS, London; **26** National Trust Photographic Library/Andrew Butler; **27** Marion Nickig; **28–29** Christopher Bradley-Hole; **30 top** Corbis/ Ansel Adams Publishing Rights Trust; **30 centre** Christopher Bradley-Hole; **30 bottom** Christopher Bradley-Hole; **31 top** © FLC/ADAGP, Paris, and DACS, London 2004; **31 bottom** Corbis/ © Alinari Archives; **32** Architectural Review; **33** gardenphotos.nl/M. Heuff; **34** akg-images, London; **35** Bridgeman Art Library/Galleria Nazionale delle Marche, Urbino; **36** Clive Nichols Garden Pictures/Design: Christopher Bradley-Hole; **37** Dieter Kienast, Swiss Re in Rüschlikon, Centre for Global Dialogue. © Vogt Landscape Architects/Jürg Waldmeier; **38–39** Peter Walker and Partners/Alan Ward; **40** View/© Peter Cook/Architect: Allies & Morrison; **41** Christopher Bradley-Hole; **42** Jacques Coulon, Landscape Architect/Photo: Gérard Dufresne; **43** Michel Desvigne and Christine Dalnoky, Landscape Architects/Photo: Gérard Dufresne; **44** Hélène Binet; **45** akg-images, London/Dieter E Hoppe; **46–47** Harpur Garden Library/Jerry Harpur/Design: Christopher Bradley-Hole; **48–49** Christopher Bradley-Hole; **50–51** The Interior Archive/Mark Luscombe-Whyte (Architect: Luis Barragan/ San Cristobal/© Barragan Foundation, Switzerland/DACS 2004; **52–53** Nicola Browne/ Design: Teresa Gali-Izard, Girona; **54–55** Helen Fickling/Design: Christopher Bradley-Hole; **56** Christopher Bradley-Hole; **57** Helen Fickling/ Design: Christopher Bradley-Hole; **58** © T. Delaney/ SEAM Studio 2003; **59** Marianne Majerus/Design: Christopher Bradley-Hole; **60–61** Martha Schwartz; **62–63** Lodewijk Baljon Landschapsarchitecten; **64 top** Desmond Lavery/Design: Christopher

Bradley-Hole; **64 bottom** Christopher Bradley-Hole; **65–67** Harpur Garden Library/Jerry Harpur/ Design: Christopher Bradley-Hole; **68–69** Nicola Browne/Architect: Renzo Piano/Garden design: Michel Desvigne and Christine Dalnoky; **70** Christopher Bradley-Hole; **71** Nicola Browne/Design: Steve Martino; **72** Nicola Browne/Architect: Oscar Tusquets/Garden design: Bet Figueras, Girona; **73** Harpur Garden Library/ Jerry Harpur/Design: Topher Delaney, California; **74–75** Nicola Browne/Design: Steve Martino, Phoenix, Arizona; **76** Georges Lévêque/Design: Jacques Wirtz; **77** Georges Lévêque/Design: Jacques Wirtz; **78** Georges Lévêque/Design: Jacques Wirtz; **79 top** From the Castle Howard Collection; **79 bottom** Marianne Majerus/ Design: Jacques Wirtz; **80–81 top** Harpur Garden Library/Jerry Harpur/Design: Christopher Bradley-Hole; **81 bottom** Christopher Bradley-Hole; **82–83** Harpur Garden Library/Jerry Harpur/ Design: Christopher Bradley-Hole; **84** Olin Partnership/Alex Vertikoff/© 2000 J Paul Getty Trust; **85** Olin Partnership/Tim Rue; **86** Tadao Ando Architect & Associates/Shigeo Ogawa; **87** Tadao Ando Architect & Associates/ Mitsuo Matsuoka; **88** Clive Nichols Garden Pictures/Design: Christopher Bradley-Hole; **89** View/© Peter Cook/Architect: Allies & Morrison; **90–91** Vladimir Djurovic Landscape Architecture; **92–93** Peter Walker and Partners; **94 top** Tadao Ando Architect & Associates; **94 bottom** Arcaid/ Richard Bryant; **95** Tadao Ando Architect & Associates/Shigeo Owawa; **96** Fernando Caruncho & Asoc., SL/Photo: Laurence Toussaint; **97 top** Andrew Lawson Photography; **97 bottom** Tadao Ando Architect & Associates; **98 top** Vladimir Sitta and Maren Parry/Terragram Pty Ltd; **98 bottom left** Vladimir Sitta and Maren Parry/Terragram Pty Ltd/Walter Glover; **99** Sofia Brignone/© Barragan Foundation, Switzerland/ DACS 2004; **100–101** Michael Freeman; **103** Arcaid /Richard Waite; **104–105** Garden Exposures Photo Library/ Andrea Jones Location Photography/ Design: Christopher Bradley-Hole; **105** Clive Nichols Garden Pictures/Design: Christopher Bradley-Hole, *Daily Telegraph*/Rocco Forte Hotels *Living Sculpture Garden,* Chelsea Flower Show 2000; **106–107** Nicola Browne/Architect: Oscar Tusquets/ Garden design: Bet Figueras, Girona; **108** Kathryn Bradley-Hole; **109** Nicola Browne/Architect: Oscar Tusquets. Garden design: Bet Figueras, Girona; **110** Andrew Ewing; **111** Garden Picture Library/ Mayer/Le Scanff/Les Jardins de l'Imaginaire, Terrasson, France; **112–113** Andrew Lawson Photography/Design: Christopher Bradley-Hole; **114–115** Andrew Lawson Photography/ Design: Christopher Bradley-Hole; **116–117** Andrea Jones/Design Topher Delaney; **118** Clive Nichols Garden Pictures/Design: Christopher Bradley-Hole; **119 top** Nicola Browne/Design: Christopher Bradley-Hole; **119 bottom** Christopher Bradley-Hole; **120–121** Oehme, van Sweden and Associates, Inc/Richard Felber; **122** Garden Picture Library/

Steven Wooster/Design Rod Barnett; **123** Vladimir Djurovic Landscape Architecture; **124 top left** Christopher Bradley-Hole; **124–125** Andrew Lawson Photography/Design: Christopher Bradley-Hole; **125 top** Christopher Bradley-Hole; **126–127** Andrew Lawson Photography/ Design: Christopher Bradley-Hole; **128** Christopher Bradley-Hole; **129** Andrew Lawson Photography/ Design: Christopher Bradley-Hole; **130–131** Christopher Bradley-Hole; **132** Andrew Lawson Photography/Design: Christopher Bradley-Hole; **133 top** © Tate, London/© DACS 2004; **133 bottom** Christopher Bradley-Hole; **134–135** Reiner Blunck/Design: Sue Barnsley and Andrew McNally; **136–137** Harpur Garden Library/ Jerry Harpur/Design: Ulf Nordfjell, Sweden; **138–139** Harpur Garden Library/Jerry Harpur/ Design: Christopher Bradley-Hole; **140–141** Stephen Stimson Associates, Landscape Architects/ Charles Mayer; **142–144** Janis Hall, Landscape + Architecture; **145 top** Bridgeman Art Library/Private Collection; **145 bottom** Phil Sheldon; **146–147** Charles Jencks, *The Garden of Cosmic Speculation,* published by Frances Lincoln Ltd, October 2003; **148 left** Andrew Lawson Photography/Design: Christopher Bradley-Hole; **148 right** Christopher Bradley-Hole; **149** Andrew Lawson Photography/Design: Christopher Bradley-Hole; **150–151** Nicola Browne/Garden design: Steve Martino, Tucson, Arizona; **152 top** Martha Schwartz Inc/Myrzik/Jarisch; **152 bottom** Martha Schwartz Inc; **153–155** Martha Schwartz Inc/Myrzik/Jarisch; **156–157** Nicola Browne/Design: Faith Okuma, New Mexico; **158** Desmond Lavery/Design: Christopher Bradley-Hole; **159** Jim Hedrich © Hedrich Blessing; **160–161** Christopher Bradley-Hole; **162–163** Harpur Garden Library/Jerry Harpur/Design: Topher Delaney and Andrea Cochran, California; **164 top** Harpur Garden Library/Jerry Harpur/Design: Christopher Bradley-Hole; **164 bottom** Christopher Bradley-Hole; **165** Harpur Garden Library/Jerry Harpur/Design: Christopher Bradley-Hole; **166–167** Jerry Harpur/Design: Christopher Bradley-Hole; **168** Aaron Kiley; **169** Sean Kernan/Design: George Hargreaves; **170–171** Aaron Kiley; **172** Nicola Browne/Design: Christopher Bradley-Hole; **173 left** Marianne Majerus/Design: Marc Schoellen; **173 right** Søren Holmberg; **174** Georges Lévêque/Design: Jacques Wirtz; **175** Sofia Brignone; **176** Marion Nickig; **177 top** Nicola Browne/Design: Piet Oudolf; **177 bottom** Andrew Lawson Photography/ Design: Christopher Bradley-Hole; **178** Andrew Lawson Photography/Design: Piet Oudolf; **179** Nicola Browne/Design: Christopher Bradley-Hole; **180** Nicola Browne/Design: Dan Pearson; **181** Nicola Browne/Design: John Coke; **182** Harpur Garden Library/Jerry Harpur/Design: Niel Diboll, Wisconsin; **183 top** Steven Wooster; **183 bottom** Andrew Lawson Photography/ Design: Tom Stuart-Smith; **184** Harpur Garden Library/Jerry Harpur/Design: Isabelle C Greene, California; **185** Jerry Pavia Photography Inc